Series / Number 90-010

Institutional Adaptability:
Legislative Reference in Japan and the United States

NORMAN MELLER

University of Hawaii

SAGE PUBLICATIONS / Beverly Hills / London

For information address:

SAGE PUBLICATIONS, INC.
275 South Beverly Drive
Beverly Hills, California 90212

SAGE PUBLICATIONS LTD
St George's House / 44 Hatton Garden
London EC1N 8ER

International Standard Book Number 0-8039-0417-7

Library of Congress Catalog No. L.C. 74-76486

FIRST PRINTING

When citing a professional paper, please use the proper form. Remember to cite the
correct Sage Professional Paper series title and include the paper number. One of the
two following formats can be adapted (depending on the style manual used):

(1) KORNBERG, A. et al. (1973) "Legislatures and Societal Change: The Case of
Canada." Sage Research Papers in the Social Sciences (Comparative Legislative
Studies Series, No. 90-002). Beverly Hills and London: Sage Pubns.

OR

(2) Kornberg, Allan et al. 1973. *Legislatures and Societal Change: The Case of
Canada.* Sage Research Papers in the Social Sciences, vol. 1, series no. 90-002
(Comparative Legislative Studies Series). Beverly Hills and London: Sage Publications

Contents

INSTITUTIONAL ADAPTABILITY:
Legislative Reference in Japan and the United States

NORMAN MELLER

University of Hawaii

The legislature [1] is an organization interlaced with supportive services, some tending to its most fundamental requirements, others less essential, and a few catering primarily on the periphery to the whims of individual legislators. Sundry staff furnish these various forms of assistance both as individuals and in structured units (see Meller, 1973: 323-325; Clark, 1967). This paper is concerned with one of these supporting services, the legislative reference agency, as viewed from a cross-national perspective.

Reading rooms with motley library collections, overstaffed arm-chairs, and writing desks, earlier accommodated both the drowsy legislator intent on napping as well as the more energetic member seeking elucidation or at least the opportunity to catch up on his correspondence. Staffs organized to furnish legislators with factual reference and analytic research services, historically an outgrowth of the library and frequently using the same plant, arrived much later on the scene. Known by many names, and overshadowed by the Congressional Research Service of the United States, [2] in one form or another these services now exist in almost all national legislatures (Inter-Parliamentary Union, 1973a: 66). However, neither such chronology nor universality necessarily demonstrate essentiality. The changing functions of the legislature may both raise the need for new services and simultaneously make long-established services superfluous, so that age is no sure measure of indispensability. Similarly, commonality is not a certain criterion, for where the legislature of one polity has consti-

AUTHOR'S NOTE: The author wishes to acknowledge the considerate cooperation received from Directors Minoru Nagano of the Japanese Research and Legislative Reference Department and Lester S. Jayson of the Congressional Research Service, as well as the members of the staffs of both agencies too numerous to name individually, when he was in Tokyo in 1970 and in Washington, D.C., in 1971. Assistance from the University of Hawaii's Research Council helped finance the research. Essential to the undertaking of this cross-national comparative study have been the services of Miss Kyoko Uno, my research assistant in Japan.

tuted the model for another, there has also been a tendency to borrow legislative staffing patterns *holus bolus*. During the course of this paper the reader may reach his own determination on the essentiality of reference agencies to their legislatures in Japan and the United States.

Little is known empirically about the total legislative staff of a single country, or the extent to which staff behavior and product are linked to the institutions they serve rather than being generic, or even idiosyncratic. This inadequacy is not cured by the researcher ranging widely over many countries, choosing data from one or another as necessary to mount a collage of legislative personnel, complete in its comprehensiveness. Nor is the answer to be found in the searching for multinational commonalities or statistical distributions, and converting them into foundations for the building of arching theory. Not alone would the undertaking of either form of cross-national study encounter a discouraging dearth of data, but it would also face the challenge of imputing spurious comparability. It may be a fact that the clerks of the numerous legislative bodies modeled round the world on the Mother of Parliaments speak a common legislative language. But concommitantly, when preceding Mr. Speaker, the Sergeant-at-Arms of Western Samoa strides into the *Maota Fono* (Parliament Building) with silver mace balanced on his shoulder—and with torso bared to the waist, *lava lava* (kilt) and *fusi siapo* (decorated hibiscus cloth sash) concealing the traditional body tatooing which stretches from umbilicus to knees—like his many other parliamentary colleagues, is he symbolically parading the authority of the introduced legislative institution by carrying this replica of an historical bauble? Or, more significantly, is he serving to transfer the dignity of *Fa'a Samoa* (Samoan tradition) as legitimation for the self-same institution? Due to such institutional divergence and cultural differentiation, even assuming a surfeit of data, any concrete findings reached from either form of cross-national study would necessarily remain suspect, while generalizations broadened sufficiently so as to meet these methodological objections would approach banality.

One course of resolution for these difficulties is the formulation of cross-national theory without recourse to empirical data, subjecting it only to the testing of logic. While this would avoid the risk of factual refutation, it also forfeits corroboration. A diametrically opposite approach is the mounting of narrowly circumscribed factual studies of specific staff from polities selected so as best to control for variation. Incrementally, general propositions may then gradually be built on such demonstrations, and ultimately permit the erecting of empirically based, broad theory. This study represents an application of the latter approach

It is accepted as a truism that institutions adjust to their environment, such adaptation itself being one of the indicia of institutionalization (Huntington, 1968: 12). Legislative staff agencies, too, conform to the legal, political, and organizational realities of the sub-systems in which they serve. But there are risks attendant on such accommodation. While failure to adjust may cause the staff agency's demise, as witness the ill-fated Office of the Coordinator of Information of the U.S. House of Representatives, over-compensation may lead to the same end. The protective skewing of a legislative agency's services by advancing narrowly partisan, political ends has similarly resulted in the forced reorganization, if not complete elimination of that agency, upon rival political leadership's ascendancy to control of the legislature. Thus mere change is not synonymous with institutional adaptation, even when the actors consciously confuse them. Nor despite old adages, does absence of change spell certain organizational disaster, just so long as staff agencies remain successfully adjusted to their legislative sub-systems.

To the extent that legislative staff agencies are transformed from being solely technical organizations, there is a marked concern for self-maintenance (Selznick, 1957: 20). Institutional adaptation can be viewed as the process by which the legislative service agency secures its own continuity. However, when such preservation is attempted in a manner and to ends out of harmony with constitutional and political reality, the obtaining of short-term extensions of organizational life is not to be confused with long-run institutional adaptation.

The American and Japanese staff agencies which provide the empirical base for this comparative study are the largest, most complete, and (with minor qualification in respect to Japan) the oldest national legislative reference services in the world. The Research & Legislation Reference Department (*Chosa Oyobi Rippo Kosa Kyoku*) of the Japanese National Diet Library represents an organization originally patterned closely on the Congressional Research Service of the United States Library of Congress, and designed to provide the same character of legislative support. But there the parallelism of the two agencies tends to end. The divergence which has occurred over the quarter of a century cannot be satisfactorily explained in simplistic, structural terms of Japan as a unitary, parliamentary monarchy distinguished from the American federal, presidential republic. The same formal dichotomization separates the United Kingdom from the United States; nevertheless, despite the marked difference between British Parliament and United States Congress (Bradshaw and Pring, 1972), the Research Division of the House of Common's Library (described in Menhennet 1970, 1965; Englefield, 1965) is assuming an ever-greater resemblance to the American CRS. [3] Rather, fundamental differences in the cultures of Japan and the United States must be looked to as sources for the variances which have today become manifest in their respective national legislative reference services.

Just as a physical organ grafted onto a living body will be sloughed off if it proves incompatible with its host, so also will inconsonant institutions borrowed from other bodies politic be rejected. Such incompatibility of social institutions is but a form of social dysfunctionalism, with the mechanisms of the polity triggered to counter introduced elements disturbing to the pre-existing homeostasis. However, as institutions possess the capacity to assume new functional roles supportive of their political systems, by doing so they may accommodate themselves to their foster environments. Precisely this is what occurred when a legislative reference service cut to an inappropriate foreign pattern was established on Japanese soil. Meanwhile, during the course of the American-induced implant's adaptation, the Japanese culture, with its greater tolerance of administrative ambiguity, added its own distinctive shape to the bureaucratization of the Diet's evolving reference agency.

This study, then, constitutes a cross-national, empirical comparison of two legislative service agencies with a common heritage and numerous formal similarities, but basic divergencies significantly linked to fundamental differences in their respective polities. It also represents a study of adaptation, highlighting within a narrow political frame the processes of institutional adjustment. Focusing its examination upon but two reference agencies, its factual findings are intended to cast light upon the mores and practices of legislative staff generically, as well as facilitate the evolving of general theory on political accommodation within the legislative sub-system.

HISTORICAL PREMISES OF THE JAPANESE R & LRD

The Japanese Research and Legislative Reference Department was interjected into the Japanese political system at the behest of the General Headquarters of the Occupation Forces. While the Diet under the Meiji Constitution was fundamentally an advisory body which attempted to check the actions of the executive, the Post-World War II Constitution raised the Diet to the central core of government (Ike, 1957: 68). GHQ's objective was to insure a representative political system, with power lodged in the Diet. To prevent the return of "shadow government," the individual Diet Member, as distinguished from those who comprised the Cabinet, required self-sufficiency and personal confidence. One of the devices adopted for thus shoring up the Diet, and contributing to representative government, was the establishment of the National Diet Library with its research and reference arm, modeled on the United States Library of Congress. [4]

Bills for creating a single library to service the Diet were presented late in 1946, and a Diet Library law was adopted in March of 1947, shortly after enactment of major legislation restructuring the Diet. [5] This embryonic library law proved too vague and perfunctory, and GHQ arranged for American consultants, headed by the Chief Assistant Librarian of Congress, to visit Japan. After their collaboration with the concerned Diet committees and other pertinent organizations, the National Diet Library Law was drafted and passed by unanimous vote of both Houses of the Diet on February 4, 1948, the day of its introduction (Report of the U.S. Library Mission, 1948: 3).

Separate libraries had been attached to the two Houses of the Imperial Diet in 1890. Fitting the limited responsibilities of that Diet, it had little need for "exact and extensive information," so the "Diet libraries never developed either the collections or the services which might have made them vital adjuncts of a genuinely responsible legislative activity" (Report of the U.S. Library Mission, 1948: 1). As a consequence, the new National Diet Library and its R & LRD were treated as novel imports from the United States, and supported as such by their Japanese sponsors. With their establishment, they absorbed the House libraries as well as the old Imperial Library at Ueno, Tokyo, which dated back to 1872.

R & LRD CREATED

Article 15 of the National Diet Library Law [6] creates the Research and Legislative Reference Department. Literal incorporation into this Article of the major parts of former Section 203 of the U.S. Legislative Reorganization Act of 1946, [7] the law which first gave the American LRS a permanent [8] statutory basis, demonstrates the intention to provide at least the same full range of services to the Diet as the LRS was then empowered to furnish to the United States Congress. [9] Even the addition of "Research" to the name of the Japanese agency recognized that the American activities were broader than simply reference-oriented, as seemingly implied by the latter's title of "Legislative Reference Service." [10]

Art. 15 - Japanese R & LRD	*Sec. 203 - American LRS*
The functions of this department shall be as follows:	It shall be the duty of the Legislative Reference Service—
(2) Upon request, or upon its own initiative in anticipation of requests,	(2) Upon request or upon its own initiative in anticipation of requests

to gather, classify, analyze and make available in translations, indexes, digests, compilations, bulletins and otherwise, data for or bearing upon legislation, and to render such data serviceable to the Diet and to the committees and members thereof, without partisan or bureaucratic bias in selection or presentation; (1) Upon request, to advise and assist any committee of the Diet in the analysis, appraisal or evaluation of legislation pending before it, or of proposals submitted to the Diet by the Cabinet, and otherwise to assist in furnishing a basis for the proper determination of measures before the committee. [Note: order of subsections reversed.]	to gather, classify, analyze and make available in translations, indexes, digests, compilations, bulletins and otherwise, data for or bearing upon legislation, and to render such data serviceable to Congress, and committees and Members thereof, without partisan bias in selection or presentation; [11] (1) Upon request, to advise and assist any committee of either House or any joint committee in the analysis, appraisal, and evaluation of legislative proposals before it or of recommendations submitted to Congress, by the President or any executive agency, and otherwise to assist in furnishing a basis for the proper determination of measures before the committee. [12]

The differences incorporated into the enabling laws of the two parallel agencies have proven to be of minor consequence. The Japanese R & LRD is directed to provide a bill-drafting service for the assistance of the Diet, its committees, and members (Article 15, subs. 3). However, with the establishment of Legislative Bureaus in both Houses of the Diet, technical drafting [13] has been eschewed by the R & LRD. [14] Fitting the broader role of the Japanese National Diet Library, [15] the R & LRD is directed, where the needs of the Diet permit, to make the information which it gathers available to other branches of the national government and the public. This authorizes the Japanese agency to have more direct service contact external to the legislature than the American LRS. [16] In fact, though, the tremendous volume of "constituent" requests handled by the latter for Congressmen has resulted in this legalistic distinction being of little significance. [17]

GIIN-RIPPO (MEMBER-LAW)

The growth of the LRS activities in the United States was closely linked with the free-wheeling role enjoyed by the individual Congressman particularly in his proposing and consideration of legislation. [18]   Similarly, the Japanese R & LRD was conceived of as encouraging Diet Members to be more independent in their actions, facilitating them in the study of problems, and then making individual decisions in sponsoring and refining legislation before the Diet. *Giin-rippo* (literally, "Member-law") was to be instituted as part of the democratic system as practiced in the United States. But the Japanese legislative process was not to develop along the United States mode nor the Diet Member to attain an individual legislative role comparable to that of a Congressman. Neither did *giin-rippo* ever become central to the Japanese legislative process. [19]

In the Diet, unlike in the United States, the individual Member has never been the sole introducing agent. The Government actively sponsors its own measures, and they are so identified. In the first few years of the Post-War Diet, Cabinet bills predominated both among measures introduced and those enacted. Then the relative proportion of individual Member's bills began to increase, as did their ratio of success, and the institutionalization of *giin rippo* appeared in the offing. But since approximately the Twenty-second Diet Session in 1955, and the new requirement for multiple Member sponsorship, further movement has been halted. Thereafter the tendency has been toward an ever greater predominance of Cabinet bills, both absolutely and among those introduced on behalf of the majority. "Consequently, a bill sponsored by an individual Member has come to mean a bill originating in an opposition party." [20]   Cabinet-sponsored bills have particularly come to dominate in their share of total legislation enacted.

Table 1. Cabinet and Member's Bills, Japanese Diet

Session(s)	Year(s)	New Cabinet Bills as % of All Bills Introduced*	Cabinet Bills as % of All Bills Passed
1st	1947	88	95
2nd-4th	1947-48	74	86
5th-6th	1949	85	89
7th-9th	1949-50	77 (77)	80
10th-12th	1950-51	69 (66)	71
13th-14th	1951-52	72 (70)	76
15th	1952	71 (71)	64
16th-18th	1953	61 (55)	71
19th-21st	1953-55	63 (54)	81
22nd-68th	1955-68	67 (59)	90

*Starting with the 8th Diet Session in 1950, bills are carried over and this is separately reported. The figures in parentheses show *all* Cabinet bills as the percentage of *total* bills before the Diet.

Source: Computed from official records.

Given the fact that in the United States all of the administration's legislative program has to be introduced through Congressmen, and that many other bills are actually initiated within the executive departments, the Japanese Study Mission which visited the United States in 1951 concluded that the Japanese legislative system was "more or less" progressing in the same direction as the American. [21]   Accordingly, the Mission called for an expansion of the Japanese R & LRD, [22] being of the opinion that there was little difference between the functions of the Department and the American LRS with respect to the Member's legislative role. In an effort to encourage the following of the American system, for a short while thereafter the Government even adopted the policy of requesting Members to propose its measures as their own, instead of introducing Cabinet bills, but this proved unsuccessful. As the data in Table 1 demonstrate, the Cabinet has continued to dominate the legislating function, [23] which has contributed to an ever greater differentiation between the two legislative systems and has influenced the functions of their respective legislative service agencies.

The self-descriptions published by the Japanese R & LRD, as well as those by the Diet Library, emphasize the primacy of their relation to the Diet. In fact, just as in the case of the Library of Congress, the parent organization's role as the national library far transcends the significance of its legislative situs. While all divisions of the Diet Library cooperate in facilitating the work of the Diet, "it is par excellence the responsibility of the Research and Legislative Reference Department" (The National Diet Library, 1966: 7, 8). Despite the ambiguity inherent in comparing tabulations of disparate data on Member services in the Library's annual reports, they fully corroborate the Departmental preeminence (see Appendix A-1).

COMPARATIVE WORKLOADS

The annual statistics published by the American CRS of total inquiries answered now reach near-astronomical proportions, and dwarf the comparable reports of the Japanese R & LRD. However, volume during the formative first quarter century of the American agency was far more modest, and bears a reasonable historical parallelism to the initial two decades of growth of the Diet's research arm. (See Appendix A-3). The phenomenal expansion in the size of the American agency's activities was to occur later. Disregarding the disproportionate volume of work now reported by the two legislative agencies, the form of response taken by their respective services also displays considerable comparability. The parallelism is further heightened when an attempt is made to remove constituent-request servicing from the American data, since the Japanese agency has to date avoided this onerous chore. That even with constituent servicing removed the American "Documentation

Table 2. *Legislative Research Reported by Form of Reply, FY 1969*

	Docum. & Other Dupl.	Oral	Written	Total
Jap. R. & LRD	49.1%	31.0%	19.9%	100.0%
Amer. LRS				
All inquiries	69.9%	17.1%	13.0%	100.0%
Constituent inquiries removed	58.3%	30.8%	10.8%	*

*Does not equal 100% due to rounding of figures.

Source: Appendices A-2 & A-4

and Other Duplication" category remains high is partially attributable to the methodology employed in making corrective computation. [24] It also results from the Japanese agency's institutional posture, encouraging more than the mere transmission of materials when servicing requests. Given the volume threatening to overwhelm it, the American CRS has no alternative but to take refuge behind this labor-saving device.

Avoiding mere repetitions of the empowering statutory language establishing the R & LRD, [25] what does the Department officially say it actually does? "The main function of this Department is to analyze and examine bills, and to make inquiry and conduct research on domestic and foreign matters, legislative precedents, and other matters in a variety of fields, in accordance with requests received from the Diet in order to aid its deliberations. Besides this work we compile bibliographies and help in the drafting of bills for introduction in the Diet. . . . Subjects which are likely to be considered in the deliberations of government will be studied by the Department even though not specifically requested by the Diet. The results of such research will be distributed to the Members of the Diet as reference materials in aid of deliberations." [26] If reliance is placed on the Department's annual reports (see data in Appendix A-2), bill analysis constitutes a relatively small number of the recorded services, and bill drafting even less. The large share of requests responded to either orally or by the supplying of documents and other duplications suggests that reference work may be an important part of Departmental activities, particularly during legislative sessions. The Department drafts no speeches, [27] unlike its American counterpart, and therefore receives few requests made with the intent that the Departmental response will be literally or even liberally used as a Member's "Statement." [28] Its preparation of indexes, digests, and comparable other publications [29] evidences the attempt to be useful, and as in the United States CRS, [30] frequently represents the logical extensions of internal institutional activities necessary to respond to repeated inquiries for the same type of data. But most importantly, the Department's reporting of "services furnished" does not reveal the full scope of its industriousness, for the statistics fail to account for self-initiated research not subsequently embodied in some form of service externally rendered either in responding to Diet Members' specific requests or in more general publications. Especially during recesses of the Diet, much of the Department's time is spent in conducting self-proposed research work "to prepare for possible inquiries from the Diet in the future or to collect material and carry out basic studies in particular fields" (National Diet Library, 1969: 5). This hiatus in the statistical record helps cloak the divergence of the Japanese R & LRD from its American model, and the former's adaptation to fit the syncretic Japanese political system.

POST-WAR DIET DEVELOPMENTS

The reshaping of the Diet after World War II constituted the introduction of elements from a presidential into a parliamentary system, probably the most crucial (Baerwald, 1964: 271-272) of which was the subject matter committee and its jurisdiction over referred bills. With elected Councillors replacing Peers, both Houses of the Japanese Diet are organized along identical lines: presiding officers named by the membership; a fixed number of standing committees and an indeterminate number of special committees, with most of the former paralleling the cabinet and executive ministries; a secretariat to handle internal administration; and a legislative bureau for satisfying of drafting chores. The majority party designates the officers and in the House of Representatives, committee chairmen. [31] Party composition of each committee is proportionate to the party's strength in the respective House, and "typical . . . has been the appointment to the appropriate committee of Diet Members with backgrounds, if not careers, in the matching ministry or executive agency." (Maki, 1962: 96). With the institutionalizing of committees, debate in plenary session has often become perfunctory, usually confirming committee decisions (Langdon, 1967: 166), and most bills are adopted immediately on reports being made by the committee chairmen. The Diet committees now represent the chief forum for party clashes, for questioning the Government not only on the substance of the bills before them but also on its political and administrative measures on a wide range of tangentially related matters. In effect, the committee stage for Cabinet bills is one of political education of the electorate, communication, and (potentially) consensus-building between parties, while for Member bills it constitutes their death knell.

PARTY ROLE

Post-war legislative development in Japan early saw management of the Diet pass into the hands of the political parties. Phrased in dramatic hyperbole, "every action is a party action, every vote a party vote, every decision a party decision. The individual member stands for nothing. Bills and resolutions, motions of any kind, speeches, interpellations, filibustering, even heckling and rowdyism in committee and House sessions —all are products of political parties" (Williams, 1948: 1163). Neither the open opposition tolerated within the legislative party by the English parliamentary system (Jennings, 1969: 88ff) nor the leadership exerted by the "outsider" in the American Congress (Huitt, 1961: 566) emerged to challenge party rule in the Diet. While interfactional squabbles might help to relax the discipline imposed by the party, "serious backbench insurrections against Cabinet leadership . . . are almost unknown to the Japanese Diet." (Ward, 1967: 95). Throughout the whole legislative process, party control constitutes the dominant element, but evidenced in forms appropriate to Japanese political mores.

Decision by majority does not exist in traditional processes of Japanese decision-making; rather, it represents confirmation of what has already been approved informally. The tendency is for consensus to triumph over majoritarianism, just as oligarchy tends to prevail over individual leadership (Scalapino, 1964: 83). When the majority party in the Diet employs its numerical superiority to ram through a controversial proposal, instead of reaching a position which accommodates the diversity of views being expressed, the Opposition considers it legitimate to use illegal and extra-legal means to prevent the action, and in doing so is supported by Japanese custom favoring consensus. Similarly part of Japanese mores, there is little opportunity for the parliamentary activities of the Diet Member to be individually conspicuous. Single Member sponsorship is now impossible [32]; one Member opposing a bill after introduction is rare. [33] It is as part of a political party, subject to enormous party discipline, [34] that the Member plays his role within the Diet.

Compensating—as it were—for the individual Member's limited ability to act on his own initiative in the Diet, "the elected Diet Members form the real heart of party organization and control." (Scalapino and Masumi, 1962: 54). With strong national parties, this allows the Members a major share in determining party position. [35] In the making of party policy, the Diet Member must share deliberations with representatives of interest groups and (in the case of the Liberal Democratic Party) the bureaucracy (Fukui, 1970: 87). Here disagreement is expressed and compromise reached, so that the rank-and-file Member may exert a degree of influence denied him within the Diet. But compared with his counterpart in the United States, in the legislative arena [36] the Diet Member's freedom of action is narrowly constrained [37] and, relatively, he contributes little to the shape of the policy legitimized by the Diet.

FUNCTIONAL ADAPTATION

It was to the realities of this Post-War Diet, party-dominated and tradition-circumscribed, that the Research and Legislative Reference Department adapted itself. Initially, in the absence of other research collections and organizations capable of servicing the Diet, a wide range of requests was received, although volume was sufficiently minimal as to encourage the Department's contacting of the Diet Members to solicit work. As objective, factual-type reporting became readily available to the Members from various competing sources with research capabilities, the Department placed ever greater emphasis upon broad-gauge, analytic studies, while the total number of requests serviced continued to grow. If it had established close working ties with the standing committees, the Department might have become more central to the legislative process. However, the committees had their own "reference staffs," headed by specialists, and after the first few years [38] the R & LRD found its committee requests concentrating on background reports with limited relation to the day-to-day flow of committee business. [39] Further contributing to Departmental distance from committee action, as well as to its tangential role in legislative policy-making, have been the long-time Diet control by the Conservatives and the "clientele relationships" established between the standing committees and the bureaucracy (Ward, 1967: 91). The ties between Members and the Ministries have not only given the members "access to the sources of authoritative information" (Fukui, 1970: 69) which negated need of recourse to the R & LRD, [40] but their input into the shaping of committee decisions has tended to make Departmental services peripheral. [41]

Appended to a parliamentary system which, despite its formal appendages, in fact gives limited scope to involvement of the individual Diet Member in lawmaking, the Department accommodated accordingly. It furnishes bill analysis and drafting services primarily for the minority parties; to the majority goes the bulk of its general reference servicing. It responds to requests for basic research reports received from Members of all parties, each mainly reflective of the bent of the individual Member. When occasionally it drafts a bill, the Department may find itself in the rare situation of directly affecting the course of Diet action. [42] Fundamental studies, comprehensive in character, are normally prepared with the assumption [43] that through a "filtering down" process they may ultimately influence concerned Ministries, majority or minority party policy committees, and general public opinion. And in terms of quantity, the quick references which the R & LRD provides probably have the greatest impact on the Diet's work, frequently finding form in the questions raised to Government proposals and challenges faced by the leaders of the majority. They sometimes even become the basis of the rare amendments reluctantly accepted by the majority, or of "conditions" [44] which influence the subsequent administration of the legislation after enactment.

PARTY SERVICING

By volume count of requests, [45] the minority parties call disproportionately upon the Department for services. Such numerical tabulations conceal the nature of those services, and elide the significance of the fact that majority Members, theoretically with a wealth of Governmental and Liberal-Democratic Party resources at their disposal, still make considerable use of the Department. In good part the explanation for this lies in the existence of minority factions within the L.D. Party and the fact that studious Members of its "main stream" faction are also unwilling to request or to rely wholly upon these sources. Reportedly, each of the Ministries phrases its services to the Diet to fit its respective policy position; the R & LRD response is acknowledgedly unbiased. In addition, for extensive, comprehensive studies spanning the interests of a number of Ministries, the Majority may turn to the Diet's research arm for what otherwise may prove difficult to obtain from the Government—a report both integrated and impartial. The R & LRD thus has not come to be identified negatively as the Opposition's research and reference agency,[46] although to greater or lesser degree, depending upon the particular situation, [47] it has become a mainstay of the minority parties.

It is thus to a parliamentary as distinguished from a presidential system that the R & LRD has trimmed its heritage.[48] Even though its services are couched in language meaningful for the process of legislating, in essence they are but aids for the actors engaged in the deadly serious political *shibai* (play) conducted periodically on the legislative boards, with the Japanese public as the audience. Through television camera and lengthy newspaper articles, the voters have opportunity to be fully appraised of each party clash in committee and plenary session, and at some future day to decide the winner on the issues as developed there. Facilitating the Member's background knowledge, supplemented by reference-type responses which prevent egregious errors, sharpens his challenges and adds dexterity to his parries, while generally raising the whole level of discussion to a higher plane for public edification. "When [arising from an important question raised or salient verbal jab at a legislative opponent, contributed to by work furnished him from the Department] a Diet Member is complimented on his ability or sagacity, this reflects well on the Department in making the Member look so good."[49] "Scenarios" for legislative action are structured through party study and strategy meetings, and here Departmental reports may serve as useful referents; staff members may even attend in order to brief participants, or for the purpose of analyzing and critiquing the policy committee's projected script. The neophyte Member must be aided in becoming familiar with his legislative role. "How are the new Members to become acquainted with the meaning of technical terms of finance? How can they fully understand the Government's bills so they can ask intelligent questions? This is the informative function of the Department."[50] Other staff members may employ different measures of the Department's responsibilities,[51] but whatever the perspective, it is always compatible with national parties using the Diet as a means for capturing and running the government of the nation.

Like its American preceptor, the Japanese R & LRD has had to "hurdle the most obvious obstacle—that of assisting the political process without being destroyed by it." (Carpenter, 1970: 1320). This burden has in no way been lightened by the Japanese Department's adapting its activities to its country's parliamentary system. Following the pattern set years earlier in the United States, the Department could cultivate its reputation for technical competence, impartiality, and political independence,[52] and thereby seek to establish its neutrality. But in the United States, the CRS has both its critics and defenders scattered over the whole political arena,[53] while in Japan there always exists the risk, given the Department's services continuously rendered in an adversary climate, of falling before an attack coalescing along party lines. Far more telling in the establishing of the Department's viability has been the incorporation into its research of a dimension peculiarly compatible with the total Japanese political system. Because of its introduction to the nation of an ever-changing range of foreign matters potentially pertinent to the Japanese policy scene, the Department has created so distinct a position for itself that it can probably now weather any attack brought out of political party pique.

FOREIGN-RELATED RESEARCH

Starting with the Meiji constitution, Japan has extensively borrowed political institutions and practices from the West in the course of its modernization (Scalapino, 1964). While massive in its impact, World War II and its aftermath of American-sponsored innovations represented only one more stage along an ever-continuing path of introduced political change. Signally compatible with this Japanese trenchant for adapting foreign experience has been the advent of the National Diet's research arm. For the first time there was now available an institutionalized capability for assisting policy makers in surveying the whole gamut of governmental activity throughout the world in the course of adopting and modifying foreign practices to Japanese needs.

From the founding of the Japanese R & LRD, a heavy component of its research has been concerned with foreign countries. Neither the "reference staffs" of the standing committees nor party research organs have any similar competence, so inquiries on external practices have gravitated to the R & LRD. Nor have many Ministries extensive knowledge of foreign experiences, so Diet Members could not depend upon them for such comparative data. Illustrative (but in no way exhaustive) of this distinctive function of the Department are publications it has issued on:

(1) town planning and urban land in Great Britain, U.S.A., Italy, and the U.S.S.R.;

(2) workmen's accident compensation schemes in foreign countries;

(3) child health in the U.S.S.R.;

(4) American vocational education;

(5) industrialization and agriculture in China;

(6) the Italian civil service;

(7) local government legislation in West Germany;

(8) administrative courts in France;

(9) present aspects and case work of the California Youth Authority;

(10) various studies on the European Economic Community; and

(11) a massive, fifteen volume, Foreign Labor Legislation Series, spanning the years 1953-63.

Potentially pertinent world developments are also brought to the attention of the Diet Members through a weekly [54] digest of foreign newspapers,

Overseas News Guide, and a bi-monthly publication, *Foreign Legislation.* Statistics record that, of Departmental services furnished, nearly half deal with foreign subjects,[55] but this quantification fails to measure accurate the much greater volume of time allocated to its research and reports involving foreign-related experience, or the importance attached to them. Indeed, the impression gained from speaking to a few Diet Members and service personnel from other Diet agencies [56] was that the greatest merit of the Department was seen to be this providing of information on foreign legislation and the practices of foreign countries.

Interviews in Washington, D.C., with the staff of the Congressional Research Service disclosed no comparable research interest in foreign experiences and solutions, and this but mirrored the domestic dimensions of expressed Congressional concerns.[57] In part this may be attributed, as a Japanese informant phrased it, to the United States Congressman taking "pride" in being inward-directed in his concerns and self-satisfied in arriving at his own solutions. It can also be explained by the wide diversity of American state practices, affording a range of experience to the Congressman which makes inquiries external to the United States superfluous; in contrast, the scope of the *ken* [58] governments in Japan is narrow and they tend toward uniformity, so that there is little alternative for the Diet Member but to have recourse to foreign practices. Congressional committees do travel overseas, but their depth of interest in these non-American experiences can be inversely approximated by the numerous times their reports are written by staff who remained in Washington. Apparently only in the politically sensitive areas of environmental policy have there currently been any requests for comparative studies on foreign practices which, in a limited way, parallel the Japanese demand for foreign data.

Staff Language Skills

Corresponding with this differential stance of the two national legislative service agencies with respect to foreign-related research is the concomitant language skills of their staff members and their respective use of foreign language materials. For both reasons of necessity (few externally-issued publications are in Japanese) and professional thoroughness,[59] the Japanese staff has occasion to refer extensively to foreign publications. Practically all of the senior Japanese staff—specialists and *kachō* (section heads)—who were queried on their language skills (25 responding, 6 unknown) could use English materials in conducting research (24), and two-thirds (18) reported skill in at least two other languages besides Japanese. A majority of their number (16) utilized materials written in German, 9 in French, 4 in Russian, 2 in Chinese and an equal number in Dutch; a scattering of other languages was also represented.[60] These senior staff members estimated that about half of their work assignments required reference to foreign language materials (median of the 26 responding, out of 31).[61]

At the outset of the American Legislative Reference Service it was assumed that foreign-language materials would be of concern to the Congress, this by virtue of the express language in the appropriation item authorizing translations.[62] Fifteen years later, an in-house report on Legislative Reference Service activities (Library of Congress, 1929-30) noted it to be the duty of its Foreign Law Section to make information published in foreign law books and legal documents available to Congressmen, sometimes through simple translations, other times involving extensive surveys. Fluent reading knowledge of at least two foreign languages was expected of persons employed for this purpose. But in the 40 years which have since elapsed, this section has been shifted out of the Service to the Library of Congress, and today the staff of the CRS relies almost exclusively on English-language materials, including those published by international bodies and foreign agencies. Such sources meeting the demand for foreign-related information,[63] no language competence in the handling of foreign research materials exists in the American agency comparable to that of the Japanese staff. The translation service within the CRS has not become a compensating counterweight, for it produces little translation in aid of the agency's research.[64] While the Japanese studies using foreign materials have continued to increase, in relative and possibly absolute terms those of the CRS appear to have declined.

SELF-INITIATED RESEARCH

Bulwarking this Japanese emphasis on foreign-related matters, and further contributing to the differentiation of the R & LRD from its American counterpart, has been the former's embarking extensively on self-initiated research followed by publication of the studies. Each service organization is supported by identical statutory language which expressly refers to the agency undertaking work "upon its own initiative in anticipation of requests."[65] Notwithstanding, the American LRS initially felt constrained to limit itself almost wholly to Congress-sponsored activity, and under the deluge of requests it now receives the CRS has almost no alternative but to continue to do so.[66] In contradistinction, as its very inception and on its own volition the Japanese R & LRD prepared and distributed studies to Members on economics, political subjects, and other related matters to engender interest in the services it could render to the Diet. Thereafter, as the Department grew and the number of requests received for its services mounted, self-proposed research has become more specialized and more diverse. It has continued to occupy a large proportion of Departmental attention, especially from early summer to December, when the Diet is not in session.[67]

The American legislative service arm has long been assembling materials and giving emerging problems comprehensive consideration in anticipation of requests. In addition, interviews with senior staff [68] confirm that some of the Congressional requests on which they work have their genesis in suggestions, pointing up their utility, originating in the CRS. But all of this is a far cry from the systemized, self-initiated legislative research program in Japan, which annually sees the researchers, specialists and *kachō* of a section each proposing his own research project for the coming year. Quite naturally the staff will tend to work in their specialized fields of interest, so their desires must be weighed in light of the Diet Members' needs. When agreement is reached, the plans of all sections are reviewed by the Planning Service of the R & LRD to avoid overlaps and lack of coordination between the work contemplated by the various sections. Most of this self-initiated research is related to foreign matters, with the specific subject dependent on the researcher's foreign language abilities. Normally projects are individual undertakings which may require up to a year for completion; sometimes, group projects are planned, and Department-originated research extending over several years is not unique.[69] The attention given to these analytic studies helps explain the relative disparity between the size of staff and number of requests reported serviced by the two research agencies.[70]

The fact that the American CRS does not engage in self-initiated research, and then publish the resultant findings, appears to stem from the conjoinder of two streams of Congressional opposition to such a practice: Some Congressmen fear the metamorphosis of the Service into a "brain trust" which will usurp the function of the Congress. Probably more solons hold to the view that the American agency was established to service the needs of the Congress and not to become a publishing house,[and that it should curtail its activities accordingly. The provisions added by the Legislative Reorganization Act of 1946 for the LRS recruiting senior specialists only reinforced the suspicions of the fearful Congressme When the Advanced Research Section housing the specialists commenced preparing topical studies as "Public Affairs Bulletins," which also receive distribution outside of Congress, the Legislative Reference Service came under attack. As a consequence, the series was terminated and a budgeta restriction now limits all publications of the Service. Congressmen determine if the Service's reports should be published, and whether in the

Congressional Record, as a House or Senate Document, or as a committee print.[72] More recently, these limitations have been partially relaxed and "when one topic is generating general legislative interest, one of the earliest inquiries received [73] on the subject is answered with a detailed analysis and/or a bibliography is prepared, and this reply will then be duplicated in quantities . . . in anticipation of further inquiries" (Goodrum, 1965: 65). The number of short studies so multilithed will run from 350 to 400 separate titles each year. "Although by law . . . [the CRS] cannot publicize these titles and their distribution is limited to specific individual requests from Congressional offices," over 200,000 copies have been sent out in a single year (Goodrum, 1968: 1580; Jayson, 1969: 184). The Japanese R & LRD has not been subjected to any similar limitation either in undertaking or publicizing its studies, so that it has full discretion in determining which reports—whether self-initiated or non-confidential Diet requested—will be published in its monthly (*Reference*) and bi-monthly (*Foreign Legislation*) organs, and in its Research Material Series of about ten volumes per year.

ADMINISTRATIVE ADAPTATION

Just prior to the establishment of the Japanese R & LRD, the Legislative Reorganization Act of 1946 had authorized the Librarian of the Library of Congress to employ nineteen senior specialists for a range of designated subject areas with the view to equipping Congress with a pool of independent experts, as qualified as those serving the executive upon whom the Congress then had no alternative but to rely.[74] Comparable provision was also incorporated into the Japanese law creating the R & LRD, but without express limitation as to number.[75]

The importance attached to the new positions is evidenced by the declaration in the Japanese Act that "the treatment of these specialists shall be equal to that of officials of the first rank in the Executive and Judicial branches of government."[76] In the American system, senior specialists are classed as supergrade positions under the General Schedule pay rates applicable to civil service employees, and placement of any post in those Olympian heights requires external approval.[77] In both Japan and the United States, appointments are made without regard to the general civil service laws or to political affiliation, and solely on the basis of fitness to perform the duties concerned. Nominally, senior specialists serve at the pleasure of the Librarian, but in fact their tenure approximates that of personnel under civil service.[78]

STRUCTURE

From the outset, the American LRS afforded distinctive treatment to its senior specialists. As outstanding experts in their respective fields, they were placed in a separate administrative sub-unit, the Advanced Research Division, [79] and each reported directly to the Director of the LRS. Befitting their acknowledged competence and close working relations with the Congress—particularly its committees—they were permitted wide freedom of action as they undertook the most difficult studies required of the Service. In addition, for the first few years senior specialists as a body met semi-monthly with the Director to consider matters of administrative policy and discuss research which might be of general interest. The analogy to the academic senate of an institution of higher learning, coupled with the broad character of their responsibilities being paralleled by those of the university professor to his department, introduced a strong note of academia. Physical separation, because the senior specialists had their offices in the adjacent Annex due to lack of space in the main Library of Congress building, and status separation, symbolized by the wide gap in classification between them and the division chiefs as the next closest group on the grade structure, set them apart and in the words of one critical informant, wrapped them in a "mantle of holiness." While the early trappings of academia gradually have disappeared, due to their inappropriateness,[80] the senior specialist rank in the CRS persists in carrying a freedom of action not enjoyed by research staff in lower grades.

In Japan, senior specialists were also structured separately from the subject-matter secitons [81] upon the establishment of the Diet's Research and Legislative Reference Department. They served as consultants to the Chief Librarian of the National Diet Library and also dealt with problems directly requested of them by the Diet Members. Like their counterparts in Washington, D.C., they did not perform routine reference duties. While technically they were all administratively within the Department, only some were housed physically with the Department in its separate, temporary office; the balance were located with the bulk of the Diet Library staff in the Akasaka Detached Palace, which served as the Library's home until 1961 when the Library Building was opened adjoining the Diet. Completing the parallel with the American legislative service arm, those specialists who were placed with the Department in its temporary offices occupied their own quarters, and were not intermixed with the subject-matter researchers. As the latter could easily identify the specialists working in their respective fields of interest, informally the could request assistance, but no close organizational ties bound the two.

The inclusion of specialists on the staffs of the two nations' legislative committees proceeded apart from the administrative structuring of their respective reference agencies.[82] A specialist heads the staff of a Japanese Diet standing committee, and he supervises both administration and subject matter content of the staff's work. In the United States, Congressional committee staff organization varies widely, with three patterns dominant:

(1) single director in charge of all staff, as in Japan;

(2) the clerical employees, headed up by the staff director, while the professional staff members each deal directly with the committee chairman and Congressmen; and

(3) two leaders, with the staff director supervising the professional staff and a chief clerk the clerical staff. (Patterson, 1970: 32-33; see also Robinson, 1970: 366-390; Kofmehl, 1962)

None of these became the controlling model for bringing all professionals into a closer operating relationship within the respective nation's legislative reference agency.

Over the approximately quarter of a century since senior specialists were first appointed, the American and Japanese agencies have increased in size,[83] and in both, the number of subject-matter sub-units has grown by fission to perform [84] the expanding volume of work which raised ever greater demands for diversified competency. Concomitantly, the two national agencies have brought their senior specialists into closer working relationships with the subject-matter sub-units, but have sharply diverged in the administrative provision made for structuring these specialists into their respective organizations.

SPECIALIST/GENERALIST TENSION

The optimal organizational relationship between subject matter specialist and administrator constitutes an organizational dilema perpetually laced with tension (see Etzioni, 1964: 75ff).[85] The specialist placed under a generalist administrator on any organizational chart faces the prospect of being directed in ways and to ends clearly counterindicated by his superior technical knowledge. Converting the specialist role so that he becomes a part-time administrator costs the organization and society the value of concentrated attention on his specialization. And treating both specialist and administrator as equals, and dividing responsibility functionally between them along respective lines of jurisdiction, while theoretically innovative, holds such potential for personal friction on the one hand, and lapses in organizational continuity on the other, as to be contemplated in the United States with caution.

Today, the charts of the Japanese R & LRD show research services and paralleling sections, the former headed by the senior specialists and the latter by *kachō*. In fact, interview discloses that the two are closely linked so that the specialists exercise technical subject-matter oversight while the section chiefs are responsible for all administration in their respective areas.[86] The Congressional Research Service, on the other hand, presents a transitional organization moving in the opposite direction with the separate Senior Specialists Division legally existent but its effective membership shrunk by attrition, and administration taking priority over individual specialized service. Now, for the most part, senior specialists are tied functionally or placed both functionally and physically within the subject divisions, and in addition, nearly all of the latter's chiefs are also classified as senior specialists.[87] Further obscuring the transformation which is occurring, as of the summer of 1971, in one division a senior specialist served as its deputy-chief, and a senior specialist housed in another informally [88] headed a small sub-group of analysts, with the former able to assign requests received by the division in his specialty to them if he did not himself personally undertake the work. Although CRS policy remains unstated, whatever the final organizational niche fixed for the senior specialist, the class will be retained, and greater ability to "act as an independent researcher"[89] will characteristically be permitted them than granted the analysts on staff.

The senior specialists/division chiefs of the CRS report very limited opportunity to perform research of a character appropriate to the rank of senior specialists, and difficulty in maintaining lengthy personal involvement when their services are requested by Congressional committee.[90] As chief, each assigns to division personnel the requests routed to his division, and, when necessary, discusses their scope and content with the analysts. The finished reports are then reviewed before they leave the division, normally for adequacy of subject-matter content by the chief or by an experienced member of the division, and editorially by the division chief for objectivity, suitability to the requestor's needs, and other comparable criteria. While the size of a division varies, the average staff is comprised of about thirty professional and clerical members,[91] and the supervision of their work is considerably time consuming. As summarized by one senior specialist who had previously headed several divisions on temporary tours of duty, "Really, division chiefs [despite their titles as senior specialists] are doing a different type of work than the senior specialists."

CRS senior specialists, functionally or both physically and functionally

ally placed within a division, continue to "prepare the highest level of studies bearing on legislative problems . . . assist with committee hearings, and provide consultative service as requested," [92] this all without direction or review by a division chief.[93] They have the option of returning work assigned them when other commitments preclude their assuming additional tasks. Depending upon personal volition, they attend division staff meetings, and maintain cross-communication regarding ongoing assignments with division personnel having related subject-matter interests. Technically they still report directly to the Director, but administratively they are being eased into the divisions, with a set of relationships (tailor made in each case) between senior specialist and division chief that enables the latter to have a comprehensive view of all services performed within his division's subject area of responsibility. But in the organizational transition of the CRS, as of the Summer of 1971, those specialists who were not also division chiefs did not oversee the research of other personnel —and division chiefs were so busy with this latter chore that they had relatively little time to perform in any other capacity.

The Japanese approach to incorporating senior specialists more closely into the Department's organization was to transfer to them full subject-matter responsibility without assigning them correlative administration chores.[94] As the change was reported, "The specialists of the Department have been performing important services from an independent position, but as their work has close connections with each section, and in order to make use of their experience, and to lead research, twelve 'legislative research services' have been established. Specialists are the chiefs of each service. . . . Each section (including the Coordination Section and Research Materials Section) will be placed under one of the research services and will work under the direction of its research service."[95] While senior specialists (and junior specialist, too) in a Research Service are organizationally classified higher than the *kachō,* so that there is a progression in status and concommitant deference as well as salary from *kachō* to specialist, they divide their functional responsibilities much as co-equals. The specialist gives subject-matter guidance, and is accountable for the accuracy and quality of the work produced by the research personnel of the service-section.[96] On the other hand, as requests are received they are assigned by the *kachō* among the researchers of his section and he sets deadlines and oversees completion of the work. If a request appears improper, the *kachō* will rephrase it to manageable proportions before referring it; should he find the decision difficult, he may request the advice and counsel of his paralleling senior specialist. Whether specialist or *kachō* have more frequent contact with Diet Members will depend upon their personalities as well as the particular subjects which happen to be the center of Diet interest.[97] The specialist does not assign work, nor may he direct a researcher to assist him; rather, these are details of administration. Personnel, budget, facilitative support, all are handled by the *kachō*. When annually planning the self-initiated research which will be undertaken for the ensuing year, specialist, *kachō*, and researchers of the section propose their individual projects, and then mutually agree upon the contents of the final service-section proposal before it goes to the Director for adjustment and authorization. The *kachō* will review completed work assignments, and may even rewrite them, before referral to the specialist for what, in many cases, is proforma approval. Completed reports leave the section with the signatures of researcher and specialist appended—and not the *kachō*, although very minor matters may be cleared by the *kachō* without review by the specialist.

Most R & LRD personnel interviewed in Japan intimated that they found the service-section organization ambiguous, with the organizational charting showing a separation of these units not borne out in practice. Each research service consists of only a few specialists, a section from ten researchers to half that number, so that the total personnel operating within a single subject-matter area can easily act in consort. Administratively, the section head communicates directly with the Director of the R & LRD; some of the specialists will assert their responsibility runs not to the Director but to their appointing authority, the Chief Librarian. In fact, they act as functional supervisors, with the dual supervision of specialist and *kachō* heading up under the Director.

Reasons for Specialist Restructuring

The same undertone of explanation for the organizational changes in the two legislative research agencies was encountered in the interviewing of staff in both Tokyo and Washington: money. In the Japanese R & LR the placing of the senior specialists in charge of units called research services appearing on a formal organization chart, with staff under their technical direction, enabled them to receive higher salaries. In the Americ CRS, it had become ever more difficult to retain division chiefs at the remuneration they were receiving; changing their rank to senior specialist broke the impasse by raising them into the super-grades, and increased their pay. A few of the American senior specialists interviewed referred to this in a slightly condescending tone, implying upgrading furnished a reward for occupying posts no true senior specialist would accept; on their part, some division heads/senior specialists defended the assigning of the higher rank to division heads as a class on the ground the chief "provides the most responsible activity in the CRS." Lending support to this contention was the proposal then being considered, now that the Congress and not the Civil Service Commission allocates CRS staff to the super-grades, of raising all division heads one grade above those senior specialists who have no assigned administrative duties.

Increase in remuneration hardly suffices as rationale for encompassing the full range of modifications made in restructuring the senior specialists into the two legislative research organizations. Both were becoming too large to permit a corps of experts to continue to remain formally aloof.[98] In Washington, junior personnel resented their inability to participate more closely with the seniors in common areas of specialty, not alone to learn for their own self-improvement but to ease their oppressive burden of work by recourse to the senior specialists' greater expertise and familiarity with sources of information. "Beyond this there were rumors, some confirmed, that the senior specialists were not subject to the same kind of restrictions that the rest of the staff observed . . . not only the much envied right to say 'no' to requests, but at least the implicit right to express opinions in various subtle ways, and having to account to no one for the conduct of their work. . . . Some senior specialists each year were known to do two jobs—immense jobs, but nevertheless only two jobs—this at a time when the others were under pressure to turn out work at a rate of fifteen to twenty requests a day. The disparity raised all kinds of hackels." In Tokyo, it was desired to utilize the specialist as "trainer, adviser, reviewer, and correcting authority, as well as continuing to do research of a basic, com-plex nature." Despite the paper organization, the reality of the change in Japan was to integrate the specialists into the flow of Departmental activity. The American changes, too, were designed to bring the senior specialist more closely in touch with the realities of life in the CRS, to equip the senior specialist with a better understanding of the matters which were of concern to the Congressmen.

The Future of the Specialist

In the United States, as in Japan, the senior specialist completely free of ties with a subject-matter division will probably ultimately disappear, although unique skills or breadth of some specialists' activities, as well as personal incompatability between specialist and division chief in other cases, may sometimes result in the maintenance of only a nominal struc-tural relationship. It is unlikely, however, that the Japanese experiment in dual supervision with specialist and administrator equal in their respective spheres, will ever supplant the American's filling of division chief posts with senior specialists, this irrespective of the loss to the Congress of the bulk of their expertise. The Japanese culture takes more kindly to ambiguous administrative situations: agreement is to be reached, if possible, through consensus rather than confrontation. Also, the higher status [99] accorded the specialist will normally be associated with a show of deference on the part of the *kachō,* while the former will hesitate to "push his position."[100] All of this has been reinforced by a lengthy period of socialization within the Japanese R & LRD, [101] as well as by most of the specialists having served as *kachō* before taking their higher posts.[102] This pattern of long service and internal promotion has been conducive to the Japanese assignment of subject-matter authority devoid of administrative responsibilities.

All American senior specialists and division heads with whom were discussed the Japanese specialist-generalist organizational "solution" uniformly responded negatively, sometimes politely skeptical and often openly hostile. Specialists opposed the limitation of administrative roles to reviewing the work output of the division, some saying the attempt to introduce change into the quality of the division's work without possessing administrative authority would present an untenable situation. Division chiefs responding expressed similar views, but as administrators disapproving foreclosure of their control over the quality of work produced by their divisions. Underlying such responses premised upon individual impact, there was tacit recognition that the greater involvement of the American legislative research agency with the activities of the Congress, and the massive volume of work performed, made straying from normal internal hierarchial relations, common to American administration, potentially threatening to the mission of the CRS.

What tended to be ignored in these critiques of the Japanese Department's organizational handling of its specialists was that the American CRS has continued to have a number of senior specialists with hierarchial linkages running the gamut of almost complete integration (senior specialists serving as division chiefs) to the loosest of supervisorial relationships (those specialists separately housed in the Library of Congress Annex with no functional ties to subject-matter divisions). The Diet's R & LRD had attempted to strike a balance between subject expertise and administration, compatible with Japanese status mores. The American CRS had written off the advantages of subject-matter specialization for the administrative benefits to be achieved by combining specialist and division head roles, but has yet to evolve a new permanent structure for its remaining specialists.

The Legislative Reorganization Act of 1970 calls for massive staff support by the CRS for Congressional committees. Senior specialists working singly, even if their numbers are materially augmented, cannot satisfy this Congressional mandate. It will necessitate team work, utilizing the other staff resources of the Service, and for this, close association with related subject-matter divisions becomes essential. Probably this will be resolved by the emergence of a number of specialized sub-units housed within a division, each headed by a senior or junior specialist and enjoying a degree of autonomy befitting his rank. If this is the solution adopted, in accordance with the American trenchant for clarity in the lines of authority and responsibility, and in the absence of the Japanese cultural ability to accommodate administrative ambiguity, there appears to be no alternative other than for each such specialist assuming direction of "his" unit. He and the unit will then be integrated into the work flow of the division, under the control of the senior specialist/division chief, so that the Service may speak with one voice to the Congress. And when this occurs, unlike in Japan, there will have occurred a further eroding of subject-matter expertise in favor of facilitating administration.

INSTITUTIONAL STANCES AND STAFF ATTITUDES

In various subtle ways, these differences in the nature of the activities, scope of discretion, and very roles of the American and Japanese legislative research arms in their respective political systems find reflection in their institutional stances and the attitudes of their staffs. In the American CRS, there is no question but that a Congressman's request takes precedence over internal matters, and in the spirit of facilitating the work of Congress, requests of Members have been accommodated which have little direct relation to the legislative process.[103] The Japanese R & LRD, while equally committed to aiding the process of the Diet, and to giving highest priority to Diet-instigated work, approaches its relation to Diet Members from a slightly varying perspective. When a *kachō* assigns requests to the staff of his section, he will take into account the importance and deadlines of the self-initiated research on which they are engaged, as well as those of all Diet-requested work, so that if possible the former may be accommodated while still recognizing the primacy of the latter.[104]

A senior staff member of the American CRS was unconsciously echoing the ethos of his organization when he said, "If you want to do something in the way of transferring scientific and technical information into the political process, this is the place to do it." And later, "I am very personally, emotionally involved in this thing [servicing Congress]. I may be putting my career on the line [in doing so]." Just as revealing for the Japanese Department was the comment of an equally senior member of its staff that he sought employment with the R & LRD because of the good collection of research materials available and the Department's wide scope of activity, so that he would not have to limit himself to one narrow specialty.

AMBIVALENCE IN REFERENCE WORK

A deep-rooted ambivalence is inherent in legislative reference work: on the one hand there is the researcher's desire to be in the center of action, a participant in the play of power which he senses all around him; and on the other, there is the wish to remain aloof and work detachedly and with balanced perspective, avoiding identification as a Member's or committee's man. Adding further dimension, there is the organizational desire to be of support to the sponsoring legislature, balanced by the fear that undue show of assistance will engender a greater number and range of requests than can be serviced adequately, reflecting adversely upon agency competence.

The two national legislative research arms share this ambivalence, and to the extent they have resolved it, the American has inclined toward involvement, the Japanese to withdrawal. The R & LRD tends to be more distant [105] from the Diet, Departmental staff less intimately involved in its day-to-day operations. Seldom do staff members work as closely with the committees and Members of the Diet as the senior members of the American CRS. Some of the latter have sat in on executive committee meetings, prepared background papers, briefed Congressmen, helped draft committee statements and plan hearings with committee staff and Congressional members, "lined up" witnesses and submitted questions to be asked at the hearings, participated in the writing of the committee report (including the committee's recommendations proposing statutory changes) and later were available to advise Members during debate on the floor in plenary session.[106] Liaison responsibilities with the Congressional committees are formally allocated among the American agency's senior staff, principally the division chiefs. The Japanese researchers reported no similar assignments and few personal contacts with Diet Members.[107] Given the many more numerous personal aides of Congressmen, the senior personnel of the American CRS had relatively less need to meet directly with Members. Nevertheless, the impression gained from interview is that their face-to-face contacts occurred with much greater frequency than did those of their Japanese counterparts.

ACADEMIC ORIENTATION

In referring to the Japanese Department's distance from the Diet, one staff informant opined, "The nearer you get to the Diet the more closely you become involved in policy decisions, and this leads to the corruption [108] of the Department personnel. On the other hand, if you remain too far away, the Department becomes much too academic. The present position between the two is just right." Both legislative research arms are cognizant of this risk of their research taking the form of "ivory tower" background pieces with little pertinancy to Member need, of being phrased in language and their contents mustered in form unusable for legislative action, so that they are branded as academic. But of the two agencies, the stance of the Japanese Department is far more academic, and this is reflected in the attitude of its staff. Since the American LRS was not structured for nor was it engaging in basic self-initiated research, [109] on its creation the Japanese Department looked elsewhere for examples on which to model this phase of its work. It found them in the academic disciplines of the universities and their methods for conducting research. The major pre-war research agencies, such as the former planning unit of the Manchurian Railway, also were copied, and recruitment of members from their staffs facilitated transfer of their practices. These employees were eager to engage in self-initiated projects, and Diet-requested work would be expanded by them to encompass self-originated subjects. As a result of dissatisfaction with the tendency toward scholastic research arising from this and other causes, in the early 1950's the Ministries were requested to loan personnel for two-year tours to fill top Departmental posts, this to introduce practical experience into the Department. The termination of the practice some years later marked satisfaction with the balance then reached in the Department between "action" and "think piece" research.

The academic-oriented antecedents of the Japanese R & LRD persist. For one thing, considerable interest is now expressed in engaging in cross-disciplinary research across intra-organizational lines in order to cope more adequately with the complexity of service requests. Also the Department has begun mounting its own field surveys for the gathering of basic data, with staff drawn from various disciplines, much along the lines of a university research team. These surveys have as their objectives, besides empirical findings, the achieving of cross-sectional cooperation and the improvement of staff members' research capabilities. The volume of fundamental, self-initiated studies has also continued to grow, and toward them some of the staff appear to have adopted an attitude bespeaking academia: "Doing self-initiated research, one is able to suggest his own standards and then aim his work at meeting those goals. This is a type of self-fulfillment and is thus of great value to the individual, to his own philosophy of life. . . . This is in contradistinction with receiving someone else's work request, and then having to work to meet their requirements." In all of this the practices of the American CRS diverge. Here reliance is placed almost exclusively upon data sources external to the Service, and the amassing of original data does not extend much beyond the making of phone calls or the distribution of an occasional questionnaire. No plans exist for extending the Service's research potential through such means as conducting of field research or the systematic use of cross-disciplinary research teams recruited from a number of its organizational subdivisions. While such practices are only embryonic in the Japanese agency, the attitude which prevails supports their extension. In contrast, the American CRS is too burdened with work to have time for such frills. "I am not an academic here; everything I do should be of service to the Congress" well identifies staff attitude compatibl with CRS policy. In the Japanese agency, within the constraints of ultimate service to the Diet as measured by his superiors, each individual researcher is encouraged to propose those projects which he deems most important for the Diet (and for younger staff, most conducive to improving his research abilities), a climate congenial to staff attitudes emphasizing individual standards and personal satisfaction.[110]

LOW PROFILE

Both research agencies have only unsystematized knowledge of their respective Members' general satisfaction with their services. Lacking an organized feed-back system [111] they respond to a variety of cues from legislative leaders, appropriation subcommittees, committees concerned with the administration of the national libraries of which they are a part, former staff now housed in strategic positions, and a number of other comparable sources. Normally all this is conducive to their adopting a safe posture calculated to offend no one, and this premised upon their own assumptions of what the Members probably want.[112] In the case of the American CRS, it has been the adoption of a low organizational profile while many of its more senior staff have worked closely with Congressmen, and particularly their aides and key staff of the committees on which they serve. With respect to the Japanese R & LRD, it similarly has assumed a background posture, but truly dealing with the Diet at arms' length, with fewer of its staff taking activist roles.

The services of the American agency have been designed to facilitate the individualistic activities of the Congressmen. The Japanese Diet Member never developed a comparable role, so the Japanese agency's services have been shaped to be consistent with a parliamentary system in which the legislature legitimates but normally has a minor impact on deciding policy. And in the process of adaptation, the services of the R & LRD have not alone become fitted to parliamentary practices but, with their content emphasizing foreign experience, have been neatly integrated into the Japanese political system. In their respective ways, each legislative research agency is institutionally supportive of the national body it serves, just as are their staffs.[113] For the American staff membe this tends to be one of greater personal identification, for the Japanese staff more linked with philosophical endorsement of the legislative institution, as distinguished from the Diet Members who comprise it.[114] The staffs of both are sensitive to the aggrandizement of the executive at the expense of the legislature which has occurred throughout the world, and regard the very existence of their agencies as reassurance that the legislatures they serve need not be dependent upon the executive departments for information. But this is not always synonymous with alignment with the legislative branch as against the executive. For some of the R & LRD staff, it is the Department in competition with the bureaucracy,[115] as distinguished from the political ministers or cabinet; for a few others it is a state of neutrality, taking no sides in the Diet's skirmishes with the executive.[116] In short, the attitudes of the Japanese Department staff do differ from their American colleagues, just as the activities, stance, and roles of their two agencies have diverged. Although nominally starting from the same base, in the words of a Japanese R & LRD informant, "If compared with the U.S. Congress, the National Diet is not too democratic. It was necessary to adapt the Research and Legislative Reference Department to this difference."

RETROSPECT

While helping to illuminate the process of political adaptation, this study raises a number of unanswered questions. Do all legislative service agencies adjust to their respective political sub-systems on pain of disappearance? Possibly "yes," but the judgment must remain tentative until in-depth empirical studies are undertaken of both long-lived and ill-fated agencies. Conversely, under some yet-to-be-specified circumstances, may not the legislature as an organization be conceived of as orbiting around its service agencies, rather than the obverse always being found in the legislative system's gravity field? Should such reversal in the ordering of positions appear preposterous, was not this at least partially the rationale supporting SCAP's founding of both the Japanese Research and Legislative Reference Department and the other service agencies [117] designed to work a reshaping of the Japanese legislative process? The lack of success of the American Occupation policy may be attributed to errors of computation in its political physics, miscalculations of the tenacious pull of Japan's consensus society and the consequent impossibility of structuring individual legislator orientation into that nation's political system. But in some of the island polities under American jurisdiction in the Pacific Basin, whose political systems have exhibited great malleability, it has been the legislative staff which has materially contributed to functional accretions as well as the institutionalization of the legislature (Meller, 1973: 329), lending credenc to the possibility of inverse legislative gravity systems.

The relation of staff agencies to the legislatures they serve may also be viewed from other perspectives. Do such agencies adumbrate their legislative bodies? At least to the minor extent staff employment constitutes a recognized path for legislative recruitment (Mezey, 1970: 567), tomorrow's legislature is embodied in the personnel of today's legislative staff. Are service agencies but faithful mirror images of their legislatures? There is little question but that staff will tend to reinforce particular aspects of legislative values and behavior, as protective sensitivity over legislative status, and it is not unknown for staff to sometimes outdo their legislative principals in imperiously demanding special treatment. But could not staff also be regarded as something of an inverse image, supplementing the body it serves, as it were making it operationally whole and thereby facilitating its articulation with other sub-systems as well as linkin it with the entire political system? The legislative draftsman who puts the hortatory "idea" of a new legislature into the legal form of effective statutory command, so that its terms can mesh with the machinery of administration and the process of the courts, provides his legislative client far more than the mechanical services of a scribe. May not all staff be similarly viewed as legislative complements, cumulatively binding the legislature to the body politic? And given this variety of perspectives for legislature-staff relationships, ought not adaptation itself be considered as a reciprocal process, with both staff agency and legislature continually adjusting to each other? If so, any definitive study of staff adaptation would have to partake of the nature of a differential equation, and a degree of relativity would always characterize its empirical findings.

And finally, in any empirical study such as undertaken in this paper can causal relationships ever be more than approximated? So many force were at work that it would have been impossible to describe the totality of events in the life of the Japanese Diet and also relate them all to the Japanese Research and Legislative Reference Department. Selection of data on the basis of significance was the author's contribution, and "significance" was guided by the potentiality of causation being empirica demonstrable, the best that can ever be achieved in complex situations. From the results of this cross-national comparative study, it appears that with minimal demands for research and reference being made by individu Diet Members, the Japanese R & LRD institutionally adapted by develop a distinctive (from the American), and particularly functional (for the Japanese) role. But it will never be empirically known, nor can theory establish, that the same adaptation would not have occurred if the Japan Diet Members *had* become replicas of United States Congressmen.

1. As to what is a "legislature" see Riggs, 1973: 42ff; Loewenberg, 1971: 3; Meller, 1969: vi.

2. While the name of Legislative Reference Service of the U.S. Library of Congress was only recently changed to "Congressional Research Service" (Legislative Reorganization Act of 1970, Public Law 91-510; U.S. Code, Title II, Sec. 166(2) as amended), the latter is used throughout the text except where it would be dysfunctional.

3. For listing and analysis of informational services furnished all national legislatures, including 18 pages of selective bibliography, see Inter-Parliamentary Union, 1973b.

4. Another related, although potentially competitive innovation was the institutionalizing of standing committees, each provided with qualified specialists as a matter of law. Diet Members would be aided by these "technicians working for and not against the legislative branch, who can match and offset the ministerial bureaucracy . . . " (SCAP, 1949: 165). Similarly, the legislative bureaus created for the two Houses paralleled the two Legislative Counsels of the U.S. Congress. The addition of all of this substructure may be encompassed within a wholly legal explanation: under the Meiji constitution the Emperor governed and made the law; under the new constitution the Diet is the one and only organ for legislation (the provisions for gazetting, promulgation, etc., are formal and do not detract from the legal recognition of the Diet as the sole lawmaking body). It was, as a matter of course, assumed that the Diet would be the initiator, and thus only logical that the Diet be provided as a lawmaking body with the assistance it would need. Hence the legislative bureaus in both Houses, Research and Legislative Reference Department in the Diet Library, etc.

5. For unpublished details on the American role in the founding of the National Diet Library and its Research and Legislative Reference Department, I am indebted to communications received from Paul J. Burnette, Libraries Officer with the Civil Information and Education Section of SCAP, 1947-49; Justin Williams, Legislative Division, Government Section of SCAP at the time of the U.S. Library Mission; and Vernon W. Clapp, chairman of the Mission. I remain solely responsible for the interpretation given these data appearing in this paper.

6. Law No. 5, February 9, 1948; found as Appendix A in Report of the United States Library Mission, 1948; National Diet Library Law, 1961.

7. U.S. Code, Title II, Sec. 166.

8. The American LRS was not given departmental status within the Library of Congress until the Legislative Reorganization Act of 1946. For 30 years previous, lacking statutory authorization, its continued existence was contingent on no Congressman raising a point of order at the annual budget consideration. This history contrasts with the Japanese R & LRD enjoying a firm statutory base from its inception.

9. Interviews with staff of the Japanese R & LRD who had participated in the consultations preparatory to the passage of the National Diet Library Law, and in the subsequent setting up of the National Diet Library and the R & LRD, disclosed that Library of Congress and Legislative Reference Service materials (including the Manual of the LRS) were translated into Japanese so as to facilitate the transfer to Japan of the philosophy of the American model, as well as provide a guide for the services to be performed.

10. Charles H. Brown, a member of the U.S. Library Mission, is reported as

having said to the Management Committee of the Diet Library that in America the acquiring of data for legislators "was first called reference work for the legislature, that is to say, *research and reference* [emphasis added] which can become the foundation for policy decisions." Minutes of the Management Committee, 1948: 55. The use of both "research" and "reference" in the title of the Japanese agency thus represents an attempt to identify correctly the nature of its services combining both American and Japanese experience, with the Japanese intent on expanding the limited scope of "research" then being undertaken by the LRS. In the United States, as early as 1958 the misnomer of "LRS" was being officially acknowledged. (See Griffin, 1958: 7-8).

11. Under comparable—although more restrictive—language dating back to the original appropriation to the Library of Congress for fiscal year 1915, the LRS had commenced providing reference services to the Congress.

12. Added by Legislative Reorganization Act of 1946, evidencing desire of Congress for LRS to work more closely with Congressional committees.

13. Interviews in Japan established the fact that the "bill drafting" reported by the R & LRD mainly consists of roughing out the substantive contents of a proposed measure, but that the technical legal drafting is performed elsewhere.

14. Coincident with the institution in the Library of Congress of a reference service, it was decided to structure bill drafting under the presiding officers of the Congress. (Gilbert, 1952: 2). Subsequently, the Congress tended to look askance at the LRS straying over the line and attempting to compete with the offices of the Legislative Counsel. While the LRS will perform legal research and analysis and occasionally does assist with drafting legislative proposals, officially "Services the LRS cannot provide" include "draft legislation." (Library of Congress, 1971: 8).

15. The National Diet Library also provides library services for the executive and judicial branches of the National government, including supervision of the libraries of these branches.

16. See Appendix A-2, itemizing non-legislative instituted requests serviced by the Japanese R & LRD.

17. One final difference in the two empowerment statutes is the authorization of the American LRS by the Legislative Reorganization Act of 1946 to prepare summaries and digests of legislative measures and public hearings before committees. Actually this had been performed by the LRS since 1935 under Congressional directive, and it is believed was omitted from the Japanese law in part as being superfluous (digests of measures) and in part because it potentially overlapped the functions of the Secretariat of each House. The Legislative Reorganization Act of 1970 deleted the authorization for the summarization of Congressional committee meetings, apparently concurring with the Joint Committee on Organization of the Congress that this could be better left to the committees themselves. U.S. Congress, Joint Committee, 1966: 41.

18. Indeed, the language of the LRS enabling legislation previously quoted in the text refers only to service in aid of *legislation*. It was not until the Legislative Reorganization Act of 1970 that statutory recognition was given to the fact that the Service assists Congressmen with their *representative* as distinguished from their legislative functions. (See U.S. Code, Title II, sec. 166(d)(5), as amended.)

19. Disenchantment with individual Member initiation was formalized by the January, 1955, amendment to the Diet Law requiring multiple Member sponsorship (for introduction of ordinary legislation, 20 in the House of Representatives and 10 in the House of Councillors; for bills containing appropriations, 50 and 20 respectivel

This represented partial reinstitution of pre-war procedure.

20. Fukui, 1970: 92. Note, however, the Member-sponsored bill data he cites for period spanning the 40th to 50th Diet Sessions show one-quarter was introduced by Members of the ministerial party, *op. cit.*, p. 93.

21. Interview in May, 1971, with former Associate Supreme Court Justice Toshio Irie, who headed the Diet Mission to the United States to study the American legislative system.

22. Not alone was the staff of the Japanese R & LRD doubled in 1952, but the Department was reorganized along the major lines of the organization chart of the LRS which had been brought back from the United States by the then-Director of the Department. Following American practice, subject matter divisions now facilitated specialization. However, the institution of senior specialists, also modeled on American practice, dates back to the original founding of the Department.

23. For the mechanics of initiating Cabinet bills, and the roles of party and bureaucracy, see Langdon, 1967: 168.

24. The CRS reported constituent inquiries constituted 44.6% of total work load. Subtracting them from "Documents and other Duplications" and "Written" categories in the same ratio as the two bear to each other results in the adjusted percentage distribution shown in Table B. However, the constituent inquiry component is probably under-reported, with Member inquiries actually being based on requests of constituents requiring only CRS transmission of documents and duplications.

25. Much of the literature only replicates or paraphrases the enabling legislation, as see National Diet Library, 1969b, 1-2.

26. Free translation of flyer distributed by the Department to Diet Members, National Diet Library, 1969a. See comparability with Library of Congress, 1971, or listing in Jayson, 1969: 179.

27. The explanation received for the lack of pressure on the Japanese R & LRD to engage in speech-writing was that materials supplied have to be reworked by the rank and file Member and his secretary to fit with the Member's limited knowledge on the subject. Governmental and party organs probably service the speech-making needs of leaders in the Diet.

28. Correspondingly, the Japanese R & LRD employs no "wordsmiths" for this purpose, as does the American CRS. For relative volume of American speech-writing, see "Statements" in Appendix A-4. The American CRS further classifies these speech writing services under "Non-legislative," "Legislative and other major addresses (Halls of Congress)," and "Other major addresses (outside of Halls of Congress);" for FY 1969 they accounted, respectively, for 764, 514, and 704 of the inquiries cleared.

29. E.g., since 1949 the R & LRD has annually published the *Nihon Hōrei Sakuin* (Index to Japanese Laws and Regulations in Force) and *Kokkai Tōkei Teiyō* (Statistical Abstracts of Japan); annually from 1961 the *Kaigiroku Sōsakuin* (General Index to the Diet Debates); and monthly since 1951, with Economic Planning Board, *Nihon Keizai Shiyō* (Japanese Economic Indicators). *Reference Bunken Yomoku* (Bibliography of Reference Materials), published annually from 1961, is a bibliography of materials on major problems and current issues closely related to public administration and legislation; its analogue in the United States, utilizing data processing techniques for more rapid collation and dissemination, is the *Selected Bibliographic Report* prepared by the CRS.

30. E.g., bi-weekly in the United States *The Digest of General Public Bills*

(popularly known as the *Bill Digest*) and monthly *The Legislative Status Report* on major legislation before Congress. Also see the now discontinued *State Law Index*.

31. In the House of Councillors, committee chairmanships are allocated in proportion to party strength in that House. As the Councillors have only delaying power over action taken in the House of Representatives, this helps to reduce the significance of the majority party not controlling all committee chairmanships.

32. For multiple sponsorship, see footnote 19, p. 38, supra. Introduction of Member Bills is customarily made only after party notification and securing party clearance.

33. The *Riji-kai* of the standing committee (executive group, composed of Members apportioned according to their parties' strengths, and presided over by the committee chairman) allocates the time in committee among the political parties, and each then designates which of its Members will speak. Only a minimum period is allowed for free discussion. The *Riji-kai* also works out compromises in advance of the committee meeting. For plenary sessions, the *Giin Unei Iinkai* (Diet Steering Committee), comprised of representatives of all parties, normally prepares the agenda, this "in turn usually respects the decisions of each party's Diet Strategy Committee (*Kokkai Taisaku Iinkai*)." (Baerwald, 1968: 954).

34. "[O]nce the party has decided on a position, the Diet Members are expected to give their support throughout the legislative process regardless of any personal feelings to the contrary." It is considered significant should a Member even abstain from voting, although a Member recognizes he has this option. (See Morey, 1971: 14f).

35. However, even here it probably is as member of a small leader-follower group, the primary unit of Japanese politics.

36. The Diet Member may have an even broader constituent service role, (see Morey, 1971: 15f). Only very incidentally would the activities of the Japanese R & LRD be applicable to such constituent servicing. Neither the Japanese R & LRD nor the American CRS undertake "case work" for Members.

37. As example of the Member's constricted freedom of action, an R & LRD staff member, in commenting upon the Department's receiving similar requests for services from several Members of one party, indicated that this evidenced poor party organization, the party lacking a clearance procedure. No Congressman in the United States would countenance any comparable constraint.

38. In its first few years, senior specialists of the R & LRD voluntarily attended standing committee meetings and occupied special seats reserved for them. Subsequently, attendance decreased and the special seating was terminated.

39. The R & LRD has an agreement with the House of Councillors for two-year exchanges of personnel for purposes of mutual familiarization. Departmental staff having such tours of duty in interview reported that about half of the committee work they performed while on the House staff was very comparable to that rendered by the Department.

40. Not that recourse to executive sources in the United States is uncommon. (Indeed, a recent survey indicates that in obtaining information, Congressmen may more frequently refer to the executive liaison offices and other contacts in government than use the American CRS. (See Techeron and Udall, 1970: 306). However, this has not, as in Japan, led to "a situation where the bureaucratic loyalties of committee members may outweigh their legislative responsibilities and their constitution position as members" of the Congress. (Maki, 1962: 96)

41. For small number of committee-instituted requests, see Appendix A-5.

Compare the committee component of 1.5% to 3.0% of all requests received by the R & LRD for the years 1962-69 (Appendix A-5) with the 6.7% figure reported by the American LRS for Fiscal Year 1965 (this of all inquiries answered). U.S. Congress, 1965: 1178.

42. As Appendix A-2 reveals, the Department receives few requests for bill drafting. When the Socialist Party followed the practice of introducing "counter bills" to Government measures, the volume was greater. Most staff members agreed that qualitatively the greatest influence exerted by the Department on the Diet was in preparing bills. While the vast bulk of these measures is drafted for the minority parties, and few succeed of passage, the Government may "steal" the ideas embodied and incorporate them in Cabinet bills. And there is the memory of that rare occasion, after all parties had agreed that the Department should prepare a bill for Diet consideration, when the Senior Specialist assigned to the drafting task was personally waited upon by the concerned Minister bent on making known his views.

43. Interviews with staff of the R & LRD revealed that many apparently had no preconceived explanations of the mechanics of how Departmental research influences actions of the Diet or the making of policy in the Japanese political system. Indeed, a frequent response was that the staff is not supposed to be concerned with this; its function is to prepare objective, technically competent reports in response to requests on anticipated Diet needs. The impression gained from the responses of the Diet Members contacted—admittedly not an adequate sample—is that few read Department reports, and that most "do their research by their ears."

44. The record of deliberations in committee and plenary session may be scanned by administrators and judges to determine legislative intent; like in the United States, the record may be deliberately "built" for this purpose. In addition, the Opposition may force "conditions" to be tied to Majority bills, which while not formal amendments, will be respected in their administration.

45. See Appendix A-5, and percentage comparisons of party strength with distributions of requests by parties. No comparable data on party requests are maintained for the American CRS, but "there appears to be little or no statistical difference" in the use of the CRS between the party in and the party out of power. (Goodrum, 1965: 66). See proposal of Robinson (1967: 274) to politicize the CRS by giving it separate Democratic and Republican party divisions.

46. So that it would not be impossible for an R & LRD staff member to deliver a lecture to the "mainstream" of the L.D. Party on the dissolution of factions!

47. For each minority party this would be linked with the existence of a party research organ, party policy committee, and the political sophistication of the party's Diet Members. E.g., Members of the *Komeito,* a new party deficient in all three, reportedly requested staff of the Department for informal, personal advice.

48. Even more specifically, to the Japanese version of parliamentarianism with a "one-and-one-half party system . . . one party that knows only how to govern and a half a party that knows only how to oppose." (Scalapino, 1964: 88).

49. Interview with an R & LRD staff member.

50. Interview with an R & LRD staff member.

51. As to assist Members to be more studious and more concerned with their legislative duties, briefing Members before foreign trips so they will creditably represent their nation, emphasizing the cultural over the materialistic and economic, etc.

52. "The Department is no paid lackey, nor does it so serve, just [slavishly] doing what it is requested. Materials are developed in the light of accuracy and truth

of what the staff sees." Interview with an R & LRD staff member.

53. See testimony of Congressmen before the Joint Committee on the Organization of the Congress in U.S. Congress, 1965: 598.

54. Semi-monthly when the Diet is not in session. Compare this externally oriented news service with the British House of Commons Library's short-lived *As Others See Us,* "a fortnightly series of comments extracted and translated from foreign newspapers and journals," and designed to alert Members to what foreign sources are saying about *Britain.* (Menhennet, 1970: 330).

55. Of the total R & LRD research in 1969, 47.5% was on foreign subjects; 47.2% in 1968; 48.3% in 1967; 53.3% in 1966; 49.1% in 1965. Extrapolated from Diet Library's annual reports.

56. Admittedly not a representative sample.

57. This generalization, of course, does not encompass foreign relations of other nations, including their military postures, insofar as they have impact upon the United States.

58. This in no way negates the Japanese R & LRD having to face the same technical difficulties as the American CRS, or any other research agency serving a national legislature: how to equate across non-comparable lines, as how to interrelate the experiences of *ken,* state, *land, department,* etc.

59. In basic studies, the Departmental staff prefers to utilize original materials published in foreign languages. Where the request emphasizes speed, secondary Japanese-language sources referring to foreign practices will be relied upon.

60. The personnel practices of the National Diet Library reinforce the use of foreign language materials. Researchers are hired by the R & LRD off of the library's general eligible roster. University graduates are examined in English, French, German, or Russian to be placed on this list. (Specialists are recruited directly by the Department outside of the library's general employment policies.) Once engaged, Departmental personnel take part in the Library's foreign language training programs.

61. As to be expected due to their other administrative duties, the median for *kachō* (section heads) was 30 to 40 percent, while specialists' median was higher than the estimated 50 percent. A sample of more junior researchers (21) reported they used foreign language materials about one-third of their working time.

62. As the appropriation item providing money to the Library of Congress for reference work was added as an amendment in the Senate, and concurred in by the House, it more appropriately might be said that it was the amendment's sponsors who "intended" that foreign language materials be made available to Congressmen in a form the latter could use.

63. Interestingly, in both American and Japanese research agencies, reference was made by senior personnel to their respective country's Department (Ministry) with jurisdiction over agriculture having a division charged with keeping current on agricultural developments in foreign countries, thus obviating their agencies' need of recourse to foreign language agricultural publications. No similar parallelism was encountered in other subject-matter areas.

64. Most of the activities of the CRS translation service are related to servicing requests from Congressmen for translation of letters, etc.

65. See p. 9 supra. The Legislative Reorganization Act of 1970 contains additional authorization for self-initiated services.

66. Note that the implementation of staff contemplated by the Legislative Reorganization Act of 1970 will permit the building of "a pool of experts who, on their own initiative, are capable of creating and producing new information and data

that are pertinent to the legislative business of the Congress." U.S. Congress, Joint Committee, 1966: 40. (The language of the 1966 report is cited by Kravitz (1971) as providing explanation for amendments made by the Legislative Reorganization Act of 1970.)

67. The median estimate was half of their working time devoted to self-initiated research for the 22 R & LRD senior staff (of 31 specialists and *kachō* interviewed) who responded to this item. The median response of researchers (20 out of 21) estimated a smaller proportion (little over one-fifth) so devoted, which probably reflects their more junior status, and therefore heavier reference workload.

68. One senior specialist who attempted himself to put in a request form for self-initiated work on which he was engaged, labeling it as "anticipatory," found the request form rejected as the CRS made no provision for keeping a record of such research.

69. E.g., the three-year comprehensive field survey on under- and over-population.

70. In 1969, the American CRS employed about 190 professionals, with the balance of the 300 plus listed as supporting staff. (Jayson, 1969: 183.) This compares with about 90 specialists and researchers on the staff of the Japanese R & LRD. For disparity in requests handled see Appendix A-3.

71. Not that the Japanese R & LRD disseminates its publications broadside as does a publishing house. Besides copies sent to Members, political parties, and similar Diet-related receivers, copies pass through the National Diet Library's distribution channels to libraries, foreign exchanges, etc. The Department maintains no program designed to give publicity to its publications and only rarely will they receive mention in the mass media.

72. From time to time, through joint resolution the CRS is directed by Congress to prepare a particular document that will be sold as a book by the Government Printing Office, such as the periodical revisions of The Constitution of the United States—Analysis and Interpretation. (Jayson, 1969: 181).

73. Not always duplication in response to a request. Interview disclosed that multilith studies will also be prepared in the subject matter divisions in aid of the work of the General Reference Division which, in responding to the many thousands of inquiries referred to it, receives numerous "repeats" on topical matters. As stated by one Senior Specialist in interview: "You try to figure out what is going to be the 'hot' subject, and then write a multilith so that [it can be used] . . . to respond to a whole bunch of inquiries." Sometimes summary materials are written up, duplicated, and distributed in response to request before there has been time to prepare a "multilith."

74. By the Legislative Reorganization Act of 1970, the fields were increased to 22, plus "such other broad fields as the Director [of CRS] may consider appropriate." Public Law 91-510: U.S. Code, Title II, sec. 203e, as amended.

75. Article 16, National Diet Library Law. Instead of specifying subject matter areas, as did the American Legislative Reorganization Act of 1946, the Japanese law merely authorized appointment "in the broad fields of interest which coincide with the fields of interest of the several Standing Committees of the Diet." Junior as well as senior specialists also serve in Japan, which did not become possible in the United States until after the enactment of the Legislative Reorganization Act of 1970.

76. *Ibid.* This would fix their salaries in the "special category," comparable to about Vice-Ministers in the executive civil service. The parallel language of the American Legislative Reorganization Act of 1946 is: "the grade of senior specialists

... shall not be less than the highest grade in the executive branch of the Government to which research analysts and consultants without supervisory responsibility are currently assigned." U.S. Code, Title II, sec. 203 (b)(1).

77. Approval of the Congressional Joint Committee on the Library has been substituted for that of a majority of the U.S. Civil Service Commission under the Legislative Reorganization Act of 1970. U.S. Code, Title II, Sec. 203(c)(2-B), as amended.

78. Research services of the national legislatures in Australia, Canada, West Germany, Great Britain (House of Commons), and Switzerland—all of which have been visited by the author—have not adopted the senior specialist institution.

79. Later the name of the division was changed to Senior Specialists Division. It still constitutes the only division in the CRS without a separate division chief. Instead, the Director of the CRS also serves as nominal chief of the Division (Congressional Research Service, 1972: 8).

80. Not alone because of the pressure of work load, but also the inability to recruit leading academicians due to the absence of academic fringe benefits, peer-group recognition for research conducted, and opportunity to truly specialize rather than being held out as a specialist in a broader subject-matter area than academics normally feel qualified to represent.

81. Initially the Japanese Department utilized numbers for identifying its sections, without any other distinguishing title, but each had a separate subject-matter jurisdiction.

82. While by no means identical, there is a large overlap in the research chores of professionals serving the legislators on committee and reference agency staffs. However, in Japan and the United States they remain structurally separate, in contradistinction to the German Bundestag, where in 1970 the staffs of the parliamentary committees were combined with the analyst groups of the Parliamentary Research Service to form six research divisions.

83. In 1969 the American LRS staff numbered over 300, with about 190 listed as professional, and the balance as supporting (Jayson, 1969: 183, see footnote 70). The latter figure compares with about 90 specialists and researchers contemporaneously on the staff of the Japanese R & LRD.

84. This may also be rephrased in Parkinsonian terms: that the work expands to accommodate increased staff. Interviewees in both the American and Japanese agencies repeatedly volunteered that the addition of qualified staff in a subject-matter area, followed by communication of this knowledge to the respective legislature, engendered a greater number of requests for services in that field. For other treatment of same phenomena see Meller, 1967.

85. Excluded from this analysis is the allocation of jurisdiction (1) between specialists on the basis of their respective professions, e.g., legal matters to the American Law Division and economic studies to the Division of Economics of the CRS; (2) between specialists on the basis of organizational symmetry, e.g., mercury in sword fish to the Environmental Policy Division, but the effect on human beings of mercury in sword fish to the Science Policy Division of the CRS; or (3) jointly to generalist and specialist units, and with formalized liaison between the two, e.g., general reference inquiries are routed to the Congressional Reference Division of CRS, more specific and difficult ones to the subject-matter divisions, but with the former maintaining liaison personnel with all subject-matter divisions to acquaint them of the nature of the work being done by Congressional Reference and the areas where cooperative assistance will aid all concerned.

86. On the Organization Chart of the National Diet Library, each of the following named sections is shown as an administrative sub-unit of the Research and Legislative Reference Department with the corresponding research service attached to the respective section by a dotted line: Politics and Public Administration, Judicial Affairs, Foreign Affairs, Education, Finance, Agriculture and Forestry, Trade and Industry, Land Development and Communications, Social Welfare, and Labor. In addition, the Research Planning Service is similarly appended to the Coordination Section, and the Overseas Information Research Service to the Research Materials Section. The Statutes and Parliamentary Document Section completes the list. (See chart insert in National Diet Library, 1966; or National Diet Library, 1969a). As the Department is distinguished by the extensive research conducted on foreign matters, the title of the Overseas Information Research Service is misleading; the latter's primary function is to publish summary accounts of articles appearing in foreign newspapers of interest to Diet Members.

87. In the Summer of 1971, when interviews were made in Washington, of the nine subject-matter divisions (Congressional Reference Division, Government and General Research Division, American Law Division, Economics Division, Education and Public Welfare Division, Environmental Policy Division, Foreign Affairs Division, Library Services Division, and Science Policy Research Division) only two had a chief who was not a senior specialist (CRD and LSD). An acting-chief, also not a senior specialist, headed another division (G & GRD). Earlier in the history of the CRS, senior specialists had sometimes served as division chiefs, but normally temporarily, as a matter of personal administrative accommodation, and they retained their role identification with the senior specialists. The CRS now states that the "research divisions are headed by a chief who also carries the rank of senior specialist." (Congressional Research Service, 1972: 8). Today, persons appointed as division chiefs/senior specialists are a group apart.

88. "Informally" in that any leadership exercised was by virtue of his acknowledged expertise. He did not administratively supervise the analysts of the group, nor did he review their work for subject-matter competence or conformance with CRS policy.

89. Staff of the CRS when interviewed frequently used this phrase as characterizing the work of the senior specialist.

90. The chief of the Canadian Research Branch has well indicated how distinctive is this personal involvement of the American senior specialist: "Clearly the abilities of the senior specialists at Washington would be wasted if they kept strictly to their terms of reference and worked only on projects, many of them relatively unsophisticated, assigned to the service by legislators. Although this is in theory their function, in practice they initiate projects themselves and guide the research inquiries of legislators along directions of their own choosing. As a result, the senior specialist tends to win the confidence of a select circle of legislators for whom he finds himself providing a semi-exclusive service. . . . The Canadian Research Branch is a very long way from providing research at this level, but as it grows the question as to whether it would be desirable to enlarge the service in this way will one day have to be faced." (Laundy, 1971: 14-15).

91. Jayson, 1969: 183. For Fiscal 1971, ranged from 18 in Environmental Policy to 52 in American Law (Appendix E, Congressional Research Service, 1972: 101).

92. Goodrum, 1965: 64.

93. However, written work which is likely to be reproduced is reviewed by the

office of the Coordinator of Research, primarily for conformance with CRS policy. This can include work of senior specialists.

94. That this is not a normal organizational relation for Japanese legislative staffing, see *supra*, p. 25.

95. Extracted from 1961 annual report of the National Diet Library; note on the R & LRD dated September 20, 1961.

96. Based on their experience, the specialists may also interject a note of caution regarding matters politically sensitive.

97. Of 26 senior specialists, junior specialists, and *kachō* interviewed, the median number of Diet Member contacts in the previous year was estimated at ten, with the median for each of the three categories about the same. Some senior specialists stated they attempted to meet with Diet Members when personal contact was necessary. Similarly, some *kachō* on interview interpreted their role as linkage between the R & LRD and the Diet Members, thus allowing the senior specialist freedom to undertake more basic research "undisturbed."

98. The number of specialists on staff has varied in both legislative research agencies. At the times of interview (Japan - 1970, U.S. - 1971) they numbered 13 senior specialists and 5 junior specialists in the R & LRD, and 19 senior specialists in the CRS.

99. While some *kachō* in interview did not hesitate to express their opinions of their senior specialists as supernumaries, who normally merely concurred in the reports prepared by section researchers (particularly if the *kachō* had previously indicated he reviewed and modified reports before forwarding them to the specialist for approval), nevertheless it was noted that the language they employed respectfully denoted the status attached to the senior specialist.

100. A seemingly insecure senior specialist, untypically not raised through the ranks of the R & LRD, in an interview stated he preferred not to meet Diet Members, personally, as this only meant he would receive requests which would eventually saddle the researchers of the section with more work.

101. Of the 31 specialists and *kachō* interviewed, one-third had been in the Japanese Department from its founding, and fully one-half for 19 years or more! In a few cases, service was broken by tours outside the Department. (By category, the senior specialists and *kachō* each had a median of 18 years in the Department, junior specialists less, with a median of 10 years.) In contrast, while the American agency was much older, for the 21 American senior personnel interviewed for whom comparable data is available, a median of only about 12 years of service was reported.

102. Of the 31 in the Japanese R & LRD, only 6 (19%) had come directly into specialist or *kachō* posts (nine, if the three who left and returned to either of these posts are included). This contrasts with 12 (60%) of 20 senior specialists, division chiefs, or both, having been recruited directly into the American CRS for these posts (fourteen—70%—if the two who left and returned in the capacity of senior specialist/division chief are included).

103. Only as a result of the 1970 amendments, 55 years after the founding of the LRS, was statutory authority given for the performance of those activities designed to service the representative as distinguished from the legislating duties of Congressmen.

104. Note, however, that to meet the new responsibilities assigned by the Legislative Reorganization Act of 1970, the CRS may have to remove staff from servicing Members' requests so that they may be free to undertake self-initiated studies.

105. In physical terms the reverse is true, as the Japanese R & LRD maintains an office in the Detached Library, right in the Diet Building, where Members can personally call to place their requests. The Department has no equivalent to the battery of telephone inquiry recorders of the CRS, backed by an even larger corps of "hot line" specialists (Goodrum, 1968).

106. Throughout such service the CRS staff member attempts to establish his identity as a resource, not an advocate, on call to both majority and minority, and to avoid coming under direct political control, such as is experienced by Congressional committee and personal staff. As expressed by one staff member, "It is not desirable that you become so close to a Member or a committee that you feel a proprietary interest in advancing their cause."

107. Japanese R & LRD staff personal contact with Diet Members is minimal (see note 97, p. 46, *supra*). Twenty-one junior researchers reported speaking more frequently to the Members' secretaries (20 out of 21), and at least as frequently to political parties (16 of 21).

108. The informant appeared to be using "corrupt" in two senses: on becoming involved in policy, impartiality and objectivity was lost; and with another meaning, that the Liberal Democratic Party had been in power so long that it was being corrupted in a moral sense.

109. At the time the Japanese R & LRD was founded, the American LRS mainly provided legal-related research and library reference services; the build up of research/analysis capacity in the social sciences occurred later.

110. A questionnaire response of 21 R & LRD researchers to the item "The three things I like best about my job" favored "type of work," "security of job" (each 14), and "physical working conditions" (10) over "serving the National Diet" (8). Note that in Japan "security of job" may also refer to not being transferred periodically to new jobs, and thus subjected to a variance of tasks, rather than just longevity of employment.

111. The Japanese R & LRD attempted a questionnaire survey of Diet Members but the response was so poor that the effort had to be abandoned. The hearings conducted in Washington over the latter part of the 1960's on reorganizing the Congress have produced a broader spectrum of Congressional opinion about the CRS than normally is available; even so, it is difficult to determine to what extent the views there expressed are representative of the general membership of Congress.

112. When the R & LRD editor of the *Overseas News Guide* was queried about the factor(s) which determined the inclusion of a news story, he replied, "I ask: 'What would I want to read if I were a Diet Member?' "

113. For responses of American and Japanese staffs to questions designed to probe their supportive attitudes toward their respective national legislatures, see Appendix A-6.

114. A number of Japanese R & LRD staff members indicated they did not encourage contacts with Diet Members, a few for reasons such as that the Members "do not have very high standards" or that this would increase the number of factual-type requests and constitute an added burden to the staff, which ought to be engaged in analytic work. Indicating distance from Diet Members, in unstructured interviews only about half of the senior staff members when queried on their work preferences responded most favorably for requests emanating from Diet Members, party policy committees, or both. However, this remains inconclusive, as on a questionnaire providing more junior Departmental personnel with structured choices of requestor, they identified "individual Diet Members" as first choice.

Support for the Diet as an institution, coupled with low regard for Diet Members as individuals, may be reflective of a more generally held opinion in Japan. "A popular attitude toward [Japanese] politicians is that they are corrupt, self-seeking, and uninterested in the welfare of the people." (McNelly, 1972: 127). An opinion poll taken about the period of the interviews in the R & LRD indicated the Japanese public does not believe Diet Members are playing the role expected of them. See Appendix B.

115. With the reluctance of the bureaucracy to provide data of a self-critical or confidential nature, the R & LRD's activities are both supportive of the Diet and in aid of the Opposition, part and parcel of the parliamentary system. That the same bureaucratic reluctance exists in a presidential system. (See Dechert, 1967: 185ff.)

116. Only one interviewed senior staff member in the American CRS appeared to hold to a view somewhat akin to that of the Japanese "Neutralists": that in some key subject matter areas there should essentially be a feeling of trust between the executive and Congress, and while the latter must retain its oversight function, it ought not substitute Congressional judgment for that of the department charged with subject matter responsibility.

117. Legislative counsels, specialized staffs for standing committees, etc.

References

BAERWALD, H. H. (1968) "The Diet and the Japan Korea treaty." Asian Survey 8:12 (December): 951-959.

———(1964) "Parliament and Parliamentarians in Japan." Pacific Affairs 37:3 (Fall) 271-282.

BRADSHAW, K. and D. PRING (1972) Parliament and Congress. Austin: Univ. of Texas Press.

CARPENTER, R. A. (1970) "Information for decisions in environmental policy." Science 168 (June): 1316-1322.

CLARK, C. (1967) A Survey of Legislative Services in the Fifty States. Kansas City Mo.: Citizens Conference on State Legislatures.

CONGRESSIONAL RESEARCH SERVICE (1972) Annual Report of the Congressional Research Service of the Library of Congress for Fiscal Year 1971, 92d Cong., 2d Sess. Washington, D.C.: Government Printing Office.

DECHERT, C. R. (1967) "Availability of information for congressional operations," pp. 154-203 in A. De Grazia (ed.) Congress: The First Branch of Government. Garden City, N.Y.: Doubleday.

ENGLEFIELD, D. (1965) "The House of Commons Library, London," pp. 38-44 in Library Services to the Legislature: A Symposium. Sydney: New South Wales Parliament.

ETZIONI, A. (1964) Modern Organizations. Englewood Cliffs, N.J.: Prentice-Hall.

FUKUI, H. (1970) Party in Power. Canberra: ANU Press.

GILBERT, W. C. (1952) The Legislative Reference Service—A Brief Sketch. Washington, D.C.: The Library of Congress.

GOODRUM, C. A. (1968) "Reference factory revisited." Library Journal 93:8 (April): 1577-1580.

———(1965) "The Legislative Reference Service of the United States Congress" in

N.S.W. Parliamentary Library, Library Services to the Legislature: A Symposium. Sydney: New South Wales Parliament.

GRIFFITH, E. S. (1958) The Legislative Reference Service of the Library of Congress, Committee Print, Committee on House Administration, 85th Congress.

HUITT, R. K. (1961) "The outsider in the Senate." APSR 55:3 (September): 566-575.

HUNTINGTON, S. P. (1968) Political Order in Changing Societies. New Haven: Yale Univ. Press.

IKE, N. (1957) Japanese Politics. New York: Alfred A. Knopf.

Inter-Parliamentary Union (1973a) Reports and Debates. Vol. I of the Member of Parliament: His Requirements for Information in the Modern World. Geneva: International Centre for Parliamentary Documentation.

Inter-Parliamentary Union (1973b) Synthesis of Results of the International Inquiry on the MP's Means of Information. Vol. II of the Member of Parliament: His Requirements for Information in the Modern World. Geneva: International Centre for Parliamentary Documentation.

JAYSON, L. D. (1969) "The Legislative Reference Service: research arm of the Congress." Parliamentarian 50:3 (July): 177-186.

JENNINGS, I. (1969) Parliament. Cambridge: Univ. Press.

KOFMEHL, K. (1962) Professional Staffs of Congress. West Lafayete, Ind.: Purdue.

KRAVITZ, W. (1971) "The Congressional Research Service and the Legislative Reorganization Act of 1970." Washington, D.C.: Congressional Research Service.

LANGDON, F. (1967) Politics in Japan. Boston: Little, Brown.

LAUNDY, P. (1971) "The research branch of the Canadian Library of Parliament." Ottawa: Research Branch, Library of Parliament.

Library of Congress (1971) Congressional Research Service - Services to Congress. Washington, D.C.

– – –(1929-30) "Legislative Reference Service activities." Typescript in File JF522, Congressional Research Service.

LOEWENBERG, G. (1971) Modern Parliaments-Change or Decline? Chicago: Aldine, Atherton.

McNELLY, T. (1972) Contemporary Government of Japan. Boston: Houghton Mifflin.

MAKI, J. M. (1962) Government and Politics in Japan. New York: Praeger.

MELLER, N. (1973) "Legislative staff in Oceania as a focus for research" pp. 314-334 in A. Kornberg (ed.) Legislatures in Comparative Perspective. New York: David McKay Co.

– – –(1969) The Congress of Micronesia. Honolulu: Univ. of Hawaii Press.

– – –(1967) "Legislative staff services: toxin, specific, or placebo." Western Political Quarterly 22:2 (June): 381-389.

MENHENNET, D. (1970) "Inside the Commons Library." Library Association Record 72:10 (October): 329-331.

– – –(1965) "The Library of the House of Commons." The Political Quarterly 36:3 (July-September): 323-332.

MEZEY, M. (1970) "Ambition theory and the office of Congressmen." The Journal of Politics 32:3 (August): 563-579.

Minutes of the Management Committee of the Diet Library (1948) "Memorandum of American Mission for Library" in Research Division, House of Representatives, National Diet.

MOREY, R. D. (1971) "Representation role perceptions in the Japanese Diet: The

Wahlke-Eulau Framework Reexamined." Paper delivered at Annual Meeting of American Political Science Association.

National Diet Library (1969b) Research and Legislative Reference Department - Outline of Its Organization and Functions. Tokyo.

———(1969a) Chosa Oyobi Rippo Kosa Kyoku no Riyo ni Tsuite (How to make the best use of the Research and Legislative Reference Department). Tokyo.

———(1966) The National Diet Library. Tokyo.

National Diet Library Law (1961). Tokyo: National Diet Library.

PATTERSON, S. C. (1970) "The professional staffs of Congressional committees." Administrative Science Quarterly 15:1 (March): 22-37.

Report of the United States Library Mission on the Establishment of the National Diet Library of Japan (1948) Department of State Publication 3200, Far Eastern Series 27. Washington, D.C.: Government Printing Office.

RIGGS, F. W. (1973) "Some thoughts on elected national assemblies," pp. 39-93 in A. Kornberg (ed.) Legislatures in Comparative Perspective. New York: David McKay Company, Inc.

ROBINSON, J. A. (1970) "Staffing the legislature" in A. Kornberg and L. D. Musolf (ed.s) Legislatures in Developmental Perspective. Durham, N.C.: Duke Univ. Press.

———(1967) "Decision-making in Congress" in A. De Grazia (ed.) Congress: The First Branch of Government. Garden City, N.Y.: Doubleday.

SCALAPINO, R. A. (1964) "Environmental and foreign contribution—Japan" in R. E. Ward and D. A. Rustow (eds.) Political Modernization in Japan and Turkey. Princeton: Univ. Press.

——— and J. MASUMI (1962) Parties and Politics in Contemporary Japan. Berkeley: Univ. of California Press.

SCAP (1949) Political Reorientation of Japan. Vol. 1. Washington, D.C.: Government Printing Office.

SELZNICK, P. (1957) Leadership in Administration. Evanston, Ill.: Row, Peterson and Company.

TECHERON, D. G. and M. K. UDALL (1970) The Job of the Congressman. Indianapolis: The Bobbs-Merrill Co.

U.S. Congress, Joint Committee on Organization of the Congress (1966) Final Repor 89th Congress. Second Session. Washington, D.C.: Government Printing Office.

———Joint Committee on Organization of the Congress (1965) Hearings. 89th Congress. First Session. Washington, D.C.: Government Printing Office.

WARD, R. E. (1967) Japan's Political System. Englewood Cliffs, N.J.: Prentice-Hal

WILLIAMS, J. (1948) "Party politics in the new Japanese Diet." APSR 42:6 (December): 1163-1180.

APPENDIX A-1

National Diet Library Services Furnished to Diet Members

Fisc. Year	Research & Legis. Ref. Dept.					Detached Library[b]			Reference & Biblio. Division				Circulation Division			
	Oral	Doc.s and Oth.s	Writ.	Part. in Mtg.s	Total	Prov. Mat.s	Oral Serv.	Total	Srch. for Mat.s	Simple Factual Inqu.s[c]	Oth.[d]	Total	Ref.	Bor. Bks.	Used Rdg. Room	Used Carrels
1969	1165	2078	888	50	4181[a]	570	161	731	133	38	78	249	248	307	997	417
1968	1156	2098	1105	65	4424[a]	755	217	972	201	89	244	534	173	485	824	545
1967	681	970	571	17	2239[a]	432	149	581	85	31	49	165	343	498	728	589
1966	912	1295	1310	27	3544[a]	872	210	1082	149	47	55	251	405	421	884	852
1965	793	1487	1030	31	3341	820	213	1030	176	28	81	285	362	289	810	887
1964	1119	1068	1805	51	4043	728	51	779	150	27	58	235	281	430	435	787
1963					2304	548	58	606					186	912	515	1308

[a] In addition, the following "Simple References" through documents were recorded separately: 1969 - 145; 1968 - 120; 1967 - 112; 1966 - 139

[b] The Detached Library is in the Diet building, and its collection includes parliamentary materials, reference work, newspapers, etc. Total services to all users listed; data not separately reported on only Diet Members.

[c] Includes "Simple Factual Inquiries," Bibliographies, and Publication Data.

[d] Includes Designation of library repositories, Explanations on library usage, and Miscellaneous.

Source: Extrapolated from annual report of National Diet Library.

APPENDIX A-2

Services Furnished by Diet Research and Legislative Reference Department

Fisc. Year	Research by Requestor			Research by Character				Research by the Form of Reply												Simp. Ref. b	Grand Total
								Oral			Doc., Oth. Dup.			Written Replies				Partic. in Mtgs.	Total		
	Total	Diet	Oth.	Total	Bill Anal.a Res.	Gen.l Res.	Bill Draft	Diet	Oth.	Total	Diet	Oth.	Total	Reports	Bibl.	Translation	Total				
1969	4652	4181	471	4652	319	4319	14	1165	227	1392	2078	205	2283	884	38	5	927	50	4652	1593	6245
1968	4925	4424	501	4925	293	4618	14	1156	198	1354	2098	279	2377	1048	77	4	1129	65	4925	1207	6132
1967	2694	2239	455	2694	25	2659	10	681	195	876	970	241	1211	552	35	3	590	17	2694	1050	3744
1966	4108	3544	564	4108	30	4078	-	912	225	1137	1295	295	1590	1312	27	15	1354	27	4108	1310	5418
1965	4075	3341	734	4075	23	4050	2	793	509	1302	1487	200	1687	1026	29	-	1055	31	4075	*	4075
1964	4416	4043	373	4416	54	4361	1	1119	189	1308	1068	183	1251	1768	38	-	1806	51	4416	*	4416
1963	2663	2304	359	2663	65	2594	4			1850							813		2663	*	2663
1962	2119			2119	36	2071	12			1506							613		2119	*	2119
1961	2232																		2232		2232

a   The jump in Bill Analyses reported for 1968 and 1969 is mainly attributable to revision of the classificatory criteria. It still understates the number of bills analyzed, for unless the research report is wholly on a bill, the tendency is to include the service under "General Research."

b   For purposes of comparisons with years prior to 1966, "Total" and not "Grand Total" should be used. For 1966 and subsequent years, "Simple References" provided by the Overseas Information Service and the Law and Parliamentary Documents Section are counted and reported separately. Prior thereto, most were not reported at all; the few that were counted were incorporated into the various "Total" annual services reported. As only between 5 and 6 percent of the "Total" services in the years 1963-1965 are attributable to these "Simple References," augmenting the 1966-1969 "Totals" by the same percentage permits reasonably accurate comparison with prior years.

APPENDIX A-3

TOTAL INQUIRIES ANSWERED (U.S.)/SERVICES FURNISHED (JAP.)[a] BY LEGISLATIVE REFERENCE SERVICE AND RESEARCH AND LEGISLATIVE REFERENCE DEPARTMENT (RESPECTIVELY)

F.Yr.	U.S.	Jap.	F.Yr.	F.Yr.	U.S.	F.Yr.	U.S.
1915 -	296	209 -	1949	1936 -	3,966	1957 -	60,443
1916 -	831	307 -	1950	1937 -	5,271	1958 -	67,843
1917 -	1,408	722 -	1951	1938 -	6,359	1959 -	76,857
1918 -	1,144	1,079 -	1952	1939 -	6,964	1960 -	81,000
1919 -	1,091	2,504 -	1953	1940 -	10,170	1961 -	84,195
1920 -	1,764	3,106 -	1954	1941 -	12,000	1962 -	99,430
1921 -	1,221	2,512 -	1955	1942 -	13,918	1963 -	105,152
1922 -	1,238	3,634 -	1956	1943 -	12,963	1964 -	97,444 b
1923 -	1,212	3,329 -	1957	1944 -	14,736	1965 -	99,832 b
1924 -	1,487	2,682 -	1958	1945 -	17,341	1966 -	117,062 b
1925 -	1,014	2,628 -	1959	1946 -	19,732	1967 -	121,013 b
1926 -	1,140	2,106 -	1960	1947 -	22,841	1968 -	131,558 b
1927 -	1,143	2,232 -	1961	1948 -	25,704	1969 -	140,267 b
1928 -	1,726	2,119 -	1962	1949 -	29,124	1970 -	171,202 b
1929 -	2,008	2,663 -	1963	1950 -	41,602		
1930 -	2,281	4,416 -	1964	1951 -	43,549		
1931 -	1,865	4,075 -	1965	1952 -	51,076		
1932 -	2,474	5,418 -	1966	1953 -	49,463		
1933 -	2,445	3,744 -	1967	1954 -	51,588		
1934 -	2,534	6,132 -	1968	1955 -	56,666		
1935 -	2,600	6,245 -	1969	1956 -	59,425		

a   Not wholly comparable as single inquiry received may occasion several service reports.

b   Changes made in recording procedures result in totals not being fully comparable with earlier data.

Source: U.S. Congress, Joint Committee on the Organization of the Congress, *Hearings,* 89th Congress, 1st Sess., 1965; Part 7, p. 1176; subsequent U.S. data from Congressional Research Service. Japanese data extrapolated from annual reports of National Diet Library.

APPENDIX A-4

INQUIRIES CLEARED BY AMERICAN LEGISLATIVE REFERENCE SERVICE, BY FORM OF REQUEST, FY 1969

Division	Written						Documents and Duplication					Oral		
	Report or Memo	Letter	Statement	Map. Graph.	Translation	Total	Repts. (a)	Gen. Mats.	Mult. (b)	Photo-copies	Total	Phone	Cont. etc.	Total
D	13			51	1	64	20	254		66	340	369	2	371
A	2,452	11	38		1	2,502	1,175	3,298	1	12	4,486	2,860	480	3,340
CR	2,932	127	3	4	2	3,068	4,416	60,317	5,902	1,540	72,175	13,198	32	13,230
Ec	1,613	3	216	9	34	1,875	822	3,523		4	4,349	1,153	494	1,647
Ed	1,553	2	372		1	1,928	1,068	3,158			4,226	1,174	425	1,599
F	667	6	260		2	935	1,004	2,937		3	3,944	940	130	1,070
GGR	921	8	863		5,003	6,795	1,000	3,739		19	4,758	1,593	112	1,705
L	5				1	6	544	13		3	560	12	3	15
N	366		125			491	8	1,467			1,475	223	26	249
SPR	277	22	81			380	19	1,573	22	18	1,632	110	366	476
S	162	11	24	1	2	200	53	82	4	7	146	148	82	230
Total	10,961	190	1,982	65	5,046	18,244	10,129	80,361	5,929	1,672	98,091	21,780	2,152	23,932
Percent	7.8	.2	1.4	.1	3.6	13.0	7.2	57.3	4.2	1.2	69.9	15.5	1.5	17.1

(a) Previously prepared LRS reports   (b) LRS Multilithed reports requested

INQUIRIES CLEARED BY AMERICAN LEGISLATIVE REFERENCE SERVICE DIVISION, BY CONGRESSIONAL CATEGORIES, FY 1969

Division	Congressional	Percentage	Constituent	Percentage	TOTAL	Percentage
D	711	.9	64	.1	775	.6
A	7,145	9.2	3,183	5.1	10,328	7.4
CR	41,069	52.9	47,404	75.7	88,473	63.1
Ec	5,033	6.5	2,838	4.5	7,871	5.6
Ed	4,951	6.4	2,802	4.5	7,753	5.5
F	4,310	5.5	1,639	2.6	5,949	4.2
GGR	10,648	13.7	2,610	4.2	13,258	9.4
L	516	.7	65	.1	581	.4
N	1,116	1.4	1,099	1.7	2,215	1.6
SPR	1,624	2.1	864	1.4	2,488	1.8
S	523	.7	53	.1	576	.4

Division Code:
D = Office of Director
A = American Law
CR = Congressional Reference
Ec = Economics
Ed = Education
F = Foreign Affairs
GGR = Government and General
L = Library
N = Natural Resources (renamed Environmental Policy)
SPR = Science Policy
S = Senior Specialists

SEPARATE SERVICE REQUESTS RECEIVED BY DIET RESEARCH AND LEGISLATIVE REFERENCE DEPARTMENT, CALENDAR YEARS 1962-1969 [a]

	1962 Rep.	1962 Coun.	1963 Rep.	1963 Coun.	1964 Rep.	1964 Coun.	1965 Rep.	1965 Coun.	1966 Rep.	1966 Coun.	1967 Rep.	1967 Coun.	1968 Rep.	1968 Coun.	1969 Rep.	1969 Coun.
Requests from members																
majority party	283	84	298	127	375	127	420	137	399	72	340	52	440	132	270	85
minority party	529	491	567	778	862	557	677	454	575	392	806	421	1023	457	795	410
-total	-1,387-		-1,770-		-1,901-		-1,688-		-1,438-		-1,619-		-2,052-		-1,560-	
Diet																
Secretariat	9	6	31	12	13	7	16	4	17	4	21	9	13	3	7	5
Standing Comms.	19	31	21	56	25	47	18	42	23	34	17	44	16	37	13	20
Leg. Bureaus	9	11	19	14	11		18	9	7	4	11	3	2	7	4	3
former members	47		63		12		24		42		40		40		110	
-total	-132-		-216-		-115-		-131-		-131-		-145-		-118-		-162-	
Political parties [b]																
majority	30		12		18		38		17		18		11		10	
minority	86		116		72		98		99		157		120		155	
-total	-116-		-128-		-90-		-136-		-116-		-175-		-131-		-165-	
Government agencies																
Executive depts.	119		142		102		103		144		119		102		71	
other govt.	33		24		23		38		29		37		45		44	
-total	-152-		-166-		-125-		-141-		-173-		-156-		-147-		-115-	
Others	-158-		-245-		-165-		-168-		-175-		-152-		-133-		-137-	
Grand total	1,945		2,525		2,396		2,264		2,033		2,247		2,581		2,139	

PARTY STRENGTH AND MEMBER REQUESTS, IN PERCENTAGES

	1962 Rep. Str.	1962 Rep. Req.	1962 Counc. Str.	1962 Counc. Req.	1963 Rep. Str.	1963 Rep. Req.	1963 Counc. Str.	1963 Counc. Req.	1964 Rep. Str.	1964 Rep. Req.	1964 Counc. Str.	1964 Counc. Req.	1965 Rep. Str.	1965 Rep. Req.	1965 Counc. Str.	1965 Counc. Req.
Majority party	63.3	34.9	54.2	14.6	60.6	35.5	57.2	14.0	60.6	30.3	57.2	18.6	60.6	38.3	57.2	23.2
Minority parties	36.7	65.1	45.8	85.4	39.4	64.5	42.8	86.0	39.4	69.7	42.8	81.4	39.4	61.7	42.8	76.8
Total	100.0	100.0	100.0	100.0	100.0	100.0	100.0	100.0	100.0	100.0	100.0	100.0	100.0	100.0	100.0	100.0

	1966 Rep. Str.	1966 Rep. Req.	1966 Counc. Str.	1966 Counc. Req.	1967 Rep. Str.	1967 Rep. Req.	1967 Counc. Str.	1967 Counc. Req.	1968 Rep. Str.	1968 Rep. Req.	1968 Counc. Str.	1968 Counc. Req.	1969 Rep. Str.	1969 Rep. Req.	1969 Counc. Str.	1969 Counc. Req.
Majority party	60.6	41.0	56.5	15.5	57.0	29.7	56.5	11.0	57.0	30.0	56.5	20.2	57.0	25.3	54.8	17.2
Minority parties	39.4	59.0	43.5	84.5	43.0	70.3	43.5	89.0	43.0	70.0	43.5	79.8	43.0	74.7	45.2	82.8
Total	100.0	100.0	100.0	100.0	100.0	100.0	100.0	100.0	100.0	100.0	100.0	100.0	100.0	100.0	100.0	100.0

[a] Does not include requests for copies of R & LRD publications, copies of newspaper articles referred to in "Overseas News Guide," materials loaned out by Laws & Legal Documents Library, or any reference work performed in Detached Library. Note that single requests may engender more than one report, etc., so data will not correspond with that in Appendix B.

[b] As a Member may place a request for a report intended for use of his party's policy committee, party servicing is understated.

APPENDIX A-6

SUPPORTIVE ATTITUDE OF SERVICE PERSONNEL TOWARD NATIONAL LEGISLATURE

Questions asked in interview with senior personnel (specialists, division/section heads of the American Congressional Research Service (21) and Japanese Research and Legislative Reference Department (32), and responded to in questionnaires of junior personnel (17 researchers) from the latter. (Responses in percentages of those replying.)

1. There are times when it would almost seem better for the Government to take the law into its own hands rather than wait for the Congress/National Diet to act.

2. If you don't particularly agree with a law passed by the Congress/National Diet, it is all right to break it if you are circumspect in doing so and careful not to get caught.

3. If the Congress/National Diet continually passed laws that the people disagree with, it might be better to do away with the Congress/Diet altogether.

4. It would not make much difference if the constitution of the United States/ Japan were rewritten so as to reduce the powers of the Congress/National Die

5. Even though one might strongly disagree with a law, after it has been passed by the Congress/National Diet one ought to obey it.

6. One should be willing to do everything that he could to make sure that any proposal to abolish the Congress/National Diet were defeated.

	U.S. (a)	Japan: senior staff (b)	all staff (c
Question 1 - No	90%(20) d	70%(31)	72%(47)
2 - No	100%(20)	97%(31)	95%(44)
3 - No	93%(16)	84%(31)	86%(43)
4 - No	89%(18)	71%(31)	78%(45)
5 - Yes	89%(18)	97%(32)	91%(45)
6 - Yes	94%(17)	94%(32)	96%(45)

d   Figure in parenthesis indicates number of responsive replies to particular questio

Correlations: U.S. (a) with Japanese senior staff (b): $r = .55$; U.S. (a) with full Japanese staff responding (c): $r = .63$.

Source: Questions adapted from attitude survey of Iowa citizens measuring suppo toward Iowa state legislature. G. R. Boynton, S. C. Patterson, and R. D. Hedlund, "Public Support for Legislative Institutions," *Midwest Journal o Political Science,* 12:2 (May, 1968), p. 166.

APPENDIX B

DIET MEMBER ROLES - PUBLIC RESPONSES

		Expected	Actually Prevails
Question 14.	What role do you expect Members of the Diet to play? (Answer shown under "Expected.")		
Question 15.	As you view the present Diet Members, which type of Member do you think actually prevails? (Answer shown under "Actually Prevails.")		

a. Since they are representative of the whole people, they should bend every effort in service of the country.

  71.4%

  (Those who labor for the sake of whole government of the country.)

  8.8%

b. Since they are elected by voters in their electoral districts, it is desirable that they should think first of their districts.

  11.1%

  (Those who put interest of constituency first.)

  12.0%

c. Since many Diet Members are endorsed by a party, it is desirable that they follow faithfully the direction of their parties.

  6.6%

  (Those who faithfully follow the direction of their party.)

  20.5%

d. It is desirable that they think first of the business, trade unions, religious and other type groups out of which they come and whose support they receive.

  1.9%

  (Those who put the interests of the group out of which they come first.)

  14.6%

e. Since being a Member of the Diet is a vocation, it is all right if Diet Members think of their own reputations and success.

  0.7%

  (Those who are concerned with their own name and career success.)

  25.2%

f. Other, don't understand, no answer.

  8.3%   18.9%

Source: NHK Broadcast Public Opinion Polling Institute. Poll taken November 30 - December 1, 1969; broadcast March 21, 1970. Based on 2208 valid returns on a random national sample of 3200, ages 20-69, using direct interview. Published in *Gekkan Seron Chōsa* (The Japanese Opinion Research Monthly), May, 1970: pp. 73-76. (Note: order of items varied for presentation in this Appendix.)

NORMAN MELLER is Professor of Political Science at the University of Hawaii. His monograph on comparative legislative reference is premised upon the joinder of 35 years experience with American legislative servicing and his training as a Japanese language interpreter in World War II. He has been a visiting professor at the Claremont Colleges, the University of California at Berkeley, and Waseda University, and visiting fellow at Australian National University. His recent publications include "Legislative staff in Oceania as a focus for research" in Allan Kornberg (ed.) Legislatures in Comparative Perspective (McKay, 1973), and "The Congress of Micronesia—a unifying and modernizing force," Micronesica 8: 12-22 (December, 1972).

A Better Way of Getting New Information

Research, survey and policy studies that say what needs to be said—
no more, no less.

The Sage Papers Program

Eight regularly-issued original paperback series that bring, at an unusually
low cost, the timely writings and findings of the international scholarly
community. Since the material is updated on a continuing basis, each
series rapidly becomes a unique repository of vital information.

Authoritative, and frequently seminal, works that NEED to be available

- To scholars and practitioners
- In university and institutional libraries
- In departmental collections
- For classroom adoption

Sage Professional Papers

COMPARATIVE POLITICS SERIES
INTERNATIONAL STUDIES SERIES
ADMINISTRATIVE AND POLICY STUDIES SERIES
AMERICAN POLITICS SERIES
CONTEMPORARY POLITICAL SOCIOLOGY SERIES
POLITICAL ECONOMY SERIES

Sage Policy Papers

THE WASHINGTON PAPERS

Sage Research Papers

SAGE PUBLICATIONS
The Publishers of Professional Social Science
Beverly Hills • London